SHORTCUTS TO BECOMING RICH

Robert E. Shindler

Copyright © 1979, Northern Virginia Publishing Company

All rights reserved. This book, or any part thereof, may not be reproduced in whole or in part without permission in writing from publisher.

Published by:
Northern Virginia Publishing Company
Elden Street, P.O. Box 607
Herndon, Virginia 22070

Printed in the United States of America

READING THIS BOOK COULD CHANGE YOUR FINANCIAL FUTURE

Why this BIG BOOK? WHY A FULL SCALE DISCUSSION of Shortcuts To Becoming Rich? Fourteen thousand books will be published this year. Why one more? Let me explain. There are two ways to earn a big yearly income. One is to earn money, pay taxes, and invest the residual. The other is what this book is all about. Shortcuts To Becoming Rich gives you workable methods, not empty promises. Its ideas and techniques are so original that the author had to invent a whole new system for expressing them. You will notice, too, that the concept of this book has a certain overtone of risk taking or speculation. This overtome arises when a person in a free enterprise society tries to achieve financial success. The plodder's way is the safe way, a nine-to-five job, a regular paycheck, company-paid health insurance and a guaranteed (though maybe not adequate) retirement income. Some of the people you will meet in this book all turned their backs on that kind of safety. They had to. If you seek instant success you must be prepared to live with a degree of risk. We will examine this factor in more detail as we mingle later with some of the Shortcuts To Becoming Rich.

You have, I believe, that human urge for the better things in life which is the common desire of all people. You desire economic security which money alone can provide. You may desire an outlet for your talents in order that you may have the joy of creating your own riches. In Shortcuts To Becoming Rich I will show you sure fire ways, which those who use the methods will soon find ideas to unlock the doors to the solutions of their problems.

Some of my techniques are known only to a few. My reason for sharing them with you in this book is to make them known to many. For the price of this book, you'll have hundreds of thousands of dollars worth of advice, based on hundreds of hours of research. The simple steps I have set down in this book are not untested theories. They are not one man's guesses and opinions. They are proven approaches to life's situations, and they are universal methods that work like magic.

You have an admirable quality. The fact you're reading this book shows that you have the intelligence to look for tools that will help take you where you want to go. In building anything we need tools. Many people in their attempt to build a successful life forget there are tools to help them. You have not forgotten. You have, then the two basic qualities needed to realize real profit from this book: a desire for greater success, and the intelligence to select a method to help you realize that desire.

Start right now, building for the future, by using innovative step-by-step approaches as described in this book. I predict — when you digest these techniques thoroughly, it'll tap your money-making abilities and start your creative mind flowing abundantly.

ROBERT E. SHINDLER

TABLE OF CONTENTS

How to Buy a House with
No Money Down 2

How to Get a $12,000 Car Free 7

Carry All the Major Credit
Cards You Want 12

How to Open as Many Charge
Accounts as You Desire 16

Live in a $100,000 Mansion
of Your Choice 19

Have 10,000 People Selling
Your Product in 60 Days 21

How to Get a $350,000
Line of Credit..................................24

How to Stop Your Creditors 34

Are You the Missing Heir
to $12 Million Dollars............................40

How to Spend $20 and Make
$150 a Week 43

How to Start Your Own
Real Estate Company.............................46

How to Buy a Going Business
with No Cash 51

How to Buy Land No One Wants and
Lease to U.S. Government 57

New Mail Order Secret...............................61

Lease a Store in a Shopping Center 75

How to Form a Corporation...For Under $60 81

How to Become a Book Critic 86

Become a Financial Broker 94

How to Start Your Own University 107
How to Completely Disappear and
    Change Your Identity 110
Get V.I.P. Treatment Wherever You Go 112
Stop Paying Taxes . . . Legally 114
Raise $5000 in Cash on
    Your Credit Cards 116
Own a Million Dollar Corporation
    in Six Weeks 118
How to Get Loans, Capital, Mortgages from
    $1000 to $25,000 120

NOTICE: This publication is designed to provide authoritative information. It is sold with the understanding that the publisher is not engaged in rendering legal service. If legal advice is required, the services of a competent attorney should be sought.

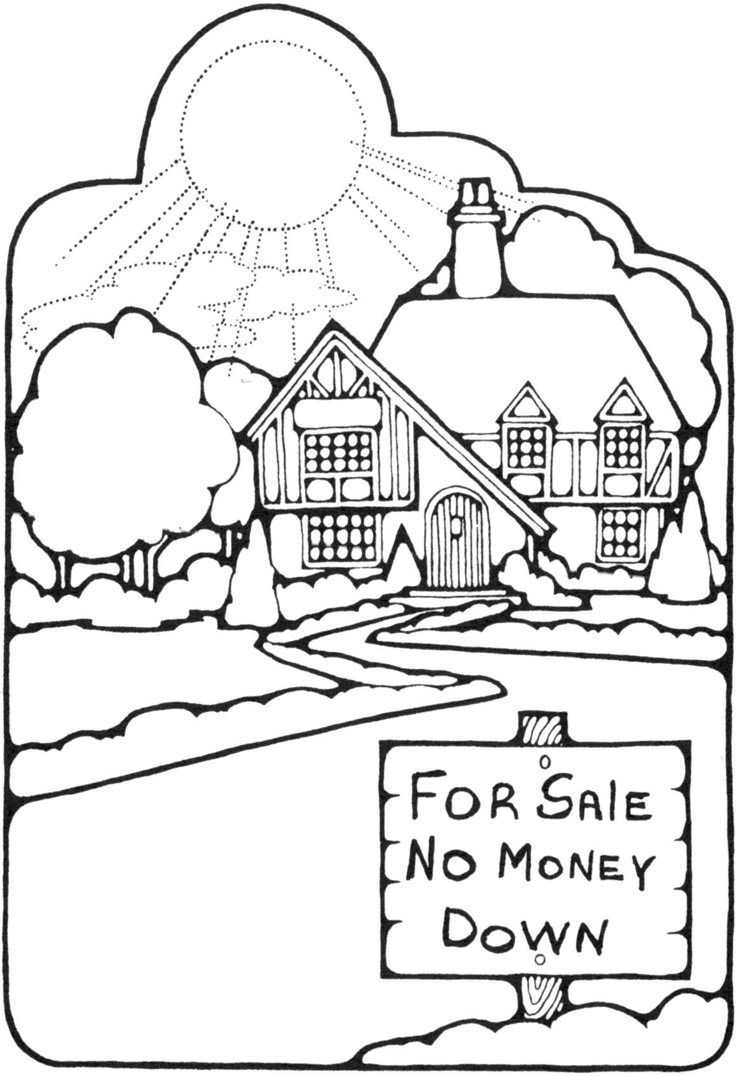
FOR SALE
NO MONEY
DOWN

How to Buy a House with No Money Down

This chapter is about an infrequently used real estate principle which when fully grasped could not only put you into your first home with no money down, but could make you independently wealthy.

It isn't necessary to spend 30 years or more acquiring riches. If you know and use the magic, smart money short-cuts in real estate described in the following chapters of this book, you can, if you apply yourself, become rich within 3 to 5 years after you begin the program. With luck, you might earn a fortune in only 3 or 4 months. Then if you wish you can continue building greater wealth or you can sit back and relax and enjoy your money. Take your choice; with money in your pocket you can afford to do so.

Buying a home by utilizing the savings of others constitutes your usual first stop as it did mine on the real estate road to a million dollars. If you own your own home you are a capitalist in the sense of owning capital along with over 70% of U.S. families according to the Federal Reserve Board figures. Most home owners borrowed from friends or family to own their own home; like 4 out of 5 home buyers who felt it was more profitable having higher house payments than at the end of the year having a handful of rent receipts. Or you might be one of the GI borrowers who match the tycoons in down payment and 100% financing. It is not uncommon to buy income property with nothing down, or 5 to 10 per cent down. I have bought about a half a million dollars worth of property with nothing down and have rejected several millions of dollars worth of property offered on the same terms.

I know of a $45,000 townhouse that recently sold for nothing down; 100% mortgage. A friend of mine bought a $250,000 25 unit apartment house with nothing down but a promissory note for $10,000. Another friend of mine bought a 45 unit building worth $645,000 by trading in as a token down payment a vacant lot that he owned worth $8,000. Of the 80% of home buyers, how many would enjoy their home ownership if they waited to pay cash? More would progress from home buying to income buying ownership if they'd only understand how much more they could accomplish with the further use of the pyramiding power of bald capital. My intent in this book is to spell out in detail how you can utilize this power open to all to make a million dollars or more.

There is no investment that has made more money for a broader segment of the population than in real estate. In particular single family homes. How many of you have made money from owning your own home? The person who has lost money from a single family residence is indeed a rarity. It's been hard to miss as the market for homes has steadily appreciated. In June of 1976 to May of 1977 the medium value of single family residents in Washington D.C. metropolitan area shot up a whopping 25%, on top of an average appreciation of 9% annually, during the preceeding five years. To have owned a home and lost money would have taken some doing for even the most incompetent investor. Those knowledgeable have made a killing.

Now, let's get on to the various techniques that you can use to achieve your ultimate goal — how to buy a house with no money down.

1. **VA Purchase** — Many people are aware of this method, but I thought I would include it for the sake of those of you who are not familiar with the benefits you may be losing by not contacting the Veterans Administration Office. If you are a veteran, the United States Government will guarantee a 100% loan for you to buy a house of your choice anywhere in this country. There is no red tape for you to go through. It is all handled by the real estate broker and your local Veterans Administration Office. Call your local VA office today to receive your Certificate of Eligibility. If you have used your VA to purchase a home in the past and have since sold it, there has been a new law enacted that will allow you to use it again. Call the nearest VA office for further details.

But I have found the quickest way to find out if you qualify to buy a home through VA is to look in the newspaper for ads for new homes for sale. In this section you will find if they have VA financing. If a particular development has VA financing just call the real estate agent and tell them that you would like to make an appointment to come out and talk to him about purchasing one of his houses under VA financing. He would be more than willing to help you because his job is to sell houses. If he can get you qualified to buy a house, believe me he will sell it.

2. **VA Houses** — You don't have to be a veteran to buy a VA house.

The Veteran's Administration Office in your local area publishes a list once a month offering repossessed houses. These are houses that were purchased under VA financing that have been repossessed because of failure to make the payments. The list contains addresses and prices and whether or not a down-payment is reqired. Most of the houses are take over payments, no money down. If you are planning to move to another part of the country, you can request a list from that part of the country to which you will be moving. In some cases, you can get a settlement before you even move.

If you don't know the address of the Veterans Administration handling your area you can write to the Veterans Administration, 941 North Capitol, N.E., Washington, D.C. 20421. You can tell them that you would like to know the name and address of the person to contact in your area to find out about the Veterans Administration sales listing. Tell them in your letter that you would like to have the Loan Guarantee Division.

3. **How to Buy a House While Including the Down Payment In the Sales Price** — The best way to work this method is to find a house that has been on the market for a long period of time, by looking back into some old classified sections of your old newspapers. But it isn't necessary for I have seen this plan work on new homes if you are dealing directly with the builder. This is an explanation of how the plan works. Explain to the owner or the builder that you have a good income and that you have never bought a home before and that you would like to sign a contract to purchase his house provided he could raise the price of the house to include the down payment and that you would like for him to pay all the closing costs. If the owner agrees to this arrangement, but he is unsure of exactly how the plan works, here is an example of the plan.

The seller writes into the contract that the down payment will be paid at closing. The buyer at that time of signing the contract gives the seller a note for $500 for the deposit. After the credit check and the approval comes back from the mortgage company, which takes about two or three weeks, the seller and the buyer set a date for settlement at either the seller's or the buyer's lawyers office. Once all of this has been arranged, you and the seller agree to exchange checks after settlement. In settlement, the attorney will ask you for the down payment (a $50,000 house selling price with 5% down equals $2,500 down). At that time you will give him a check for $2,500 drawn from your checking account. After settlement, the seller hands you a check for the same. If you have any doubts about the seller giving you his check to cover your check, don't, for if your check bounces the deal will not go through and he will be right back where he started from with his house back on the market as he wasn't able to sell.

4. **Second Trust Method** — This method is similar to the previous method except that you and the seller do not have to exchange checks, etc. You simply find an agreeable seller who will hold a second trust for the down payment. You do this by looking in your local newspaper under houses for sale. Usually in the Sunday newspaper you will find at least 5 or 6 people that are willing to take a second trust for the down payment. The reason for this is that a lot of people would rather have a second trust and avoid payment of taxes on the profit in the following year. If it is not possible for the

seller to pay the closing costs, make sure that he has included it in the second trust. This will enable you to purchase a home with no money down.

5. **Rent with an Option to Buy** — This is by far one of the easiest methods to get started owning your own home. Look in the newspaper for sellers who offer the arrangement for you to rent with the option to buy with half or all of the monthly rental being credited toward the purchase price. Usually after one year, you will have accumulated enough to go to settlement to purchase the home.

It is never too late to start. Many of my friends are cautious but are disappointed and sad today. ("I wish I were in your shoes and started investing in homes as you did. It is too late to start now.") It is never too late to start. Although fortune favors early starters; each day of delay rolls the dice against maximum odds of success. But I know many of successful owners who bought their first home after retirement at age 65. You can always start later in life and possibly with a modified financial goal. In contrast, some of my younger friends have asked, "Is it too early to get started?" In the home owners association to which I belong, some members still in their twenties are already well launched on a successful income property program. Many couples between the ages of 25 and 30 own four houses. One couple I know, the husband is 28 years old and his wife is 23, own 15 townhouses on the outskirts of Alexandria, Virginia. Their whole program was started five years before with $150 down on a townhouse that was over 85 years old. Another friend of mine that retired last year from the wage eraning 9 to 5 treadmill at the ripe old age of 35, has retired with a quarter of a million dollar estate, which he started by buying his first house under the GI program with no money down.

Anyone with the confidence to aim at the goal shown has a good chance of fulfillment. Through maximum success demands, consistent effort, the reality roads to riches requires neither superhuman endeavor or super intelligence. The chief attribute of successful reality investors are imagination, enterprise and persistence. Imagination means the vision to see the inherent potentiality of property investment. Exterprise means the willingness to venture both capital and effort in the pursuit of a worthwhile goal. Persistence means the ability to adhere to a program till the goal is achieved or surpassed.

"Miss Smith, make a note to call Mr. Elton and tell him he can pick up his free car this afternoon."

Get a $12,000 Car Free

Arriving at a friend's house or at your office in a new Cadillac or Mercedes-Benz will give a tremendous boost to your image. It will also give you a high degree of prestige in your community that will move you into the right circles of finance, making it easier to borrow large sums of cash whenever the need arises.

The plan is simple and is done with tax shelters. All that is needed is to form a corporation that is in the business of leasing automobiles.

Step One of the Plan: Set up your own automobile leasing corporation. Use a name like "American Executive Leasing Corporation;" make it impressive. Then make yourself the president and your wife the vice-president.

Step Two of the Plan: Call a Cadillac or Mercedes dealer, and tell them that you are going to be buying 10 new cars from them each year for five years, and that you are the president of (your corporation name) leasing company. Inform them you would like to have a dealer car to use with dealer tags so that you can show your prospective clients the automobile before leasing it. This will work but you must shop around and find the right dealer, one who is not selling as many as the other dealers. This will not cost him anything, so don't be afraid to ask. The car you drive is just another advertising demonstrator to the dealer, and after about 6,000 miles he will replace the car you are driving with another new one.

Step Three of the Plan: Contact professional people that are in the 50% tax bracket (heads of large corporations, lawyers, dentists, doctors, retailers who own their own business, restaurant owners, etc.). Most of these people can be found in the yellow pages or by contacting mail order houses that have mailing lists of such persons. You can either write a letter or contact the prospective clients in person or do both. Here is an example of a letter that I have found works very well.

DEAR RESTAURANT OWNER:
(Make sure you use his full name)

How would you like to drive a new $12,000 Lincoln Continental FREE every year? I will show you how. Ny name is (your name) and I am the President of "American Executive Leasing Corporation" in (your home town). We at American Executive Leasing Corporation have devised a plan using tax shelters and corporate loopholes (so that there will be no personal liability on your part) to provide you with a new luxury automobile each year for five years at no cost to you.

I'll be calling on you to give you complete details and other valuable information. Please send the enclosed self-addressed card indicating your interest. Several programs are available in your area.

Thank you,

(your name) President,
American Executive Leasing Corporation

You should have this or a similar letter printed on a nice professional letterhead. Mail the letter to at least 1000 persons who you think are in the 50% tax bracket.

Carry a portfolio or notebook with clear plastic page covers illustrating the plan, and brochures of the cars you are leasing (Lincoln, Cadiallac, Mercedes or others you might use).

Now, here is how the plan works: First set an appointment with your prospective client. At the meeting explain to him or her how the financial details of your plan works. Show them how each of 10 people are going to own 10% of the stock in the leasing corporation, and for 10% of the stock, they are going to put up $2,600.00 each, thus each having an equal share of the leasing corporation.

Remember that you can only have ten persons in your automobile leasing corporation. For if you have more than ten persons, you will be prevented from qualifying as a Sub Chapter "S" Corporation.

Here are the qualifications for forming a Sub Chapter "S" Corporation.

(Note: It is recommended that both the Federal Securities and Exchange Commission and state S.E.C. laws be checked before issuing stock in your corporation. A competent attorney will be glad to give you advice.)

1. Persons of this corporation cannot be a stockholder of any affiliated group of corporations.
2. The corporation issues one class of stock only.
3. There can be no more than 10 shareholders.
4. All shareholders must come from the same state of which the corporation is domiciled.
5. Only individuals can be stockholders. Corporations cannot be stockholders.

After locating ten individuals who will be more than willing to agree to participate as stockholders in your corporation, each one buys his share for $2,600 and you make arrangements for the cars to be delivered to each shareholder.

Now the corporation pays $26,000 down payment and borrows the balance from a local bank. After financial arrangements are made at the bank, the cars are delivered to each shareholder.

Now, let me show you how the financial part of this program works. (You should have this printed to carry in your portfolio to show each prospective client. Remember to have xerox copies made to leave with them so they may show it to their accountant. He may be your next customer.)

The cost of 10 cars wholesale
@ $9,200.00 each $92,000.00
(You will be buying the cars wholesale from the dealer with whom you are dealing.)

Ten shareholders pay @ $2,600.00 each $26,000.00

Balance to finance at local bank $66,000.00

The payments on $66,000.00 at 9% interest for 12 months are $5,767.25 per month.

$69,207.00 = 12 months
$66,000.00 = Loan amount
$ 3,207.00 = Interest on loan for one year

Each one of the stockholders will pay the corporation $576.72 per month for 12 months. At the end of 12 months each stockholder will be free and clear of all payments to said corporation.

This will be the tax advantage to each stockholder:
The corporation will receive
20% first year depreciation $1,840.00

The corporation will receive
1/10 of interest payments .... $ 320.70

The corporation will receive
1/6 of cost for depreciation $1,533.33

TOTAL $3,694.03

This is a personal write off for each stockholder. Automobile lease payments to a corporation are 100% deductible to each stockholder for business expenses...$6,920.64.

THIS IS THE TOTAL WRITE OFF THAT EACH STOCKHOLDER CAN TAKE THE FIRST YEAR. $10,614.67 less 50% to stockholders in the 50% tax bracket...$5,307.33. (All stockholders should be in the 50% tax bracket to participate.)

Each stockholder's total cash expenditure...$5,307.33. Each stockholder can keep the car ot take it back to dealer and receive approximately this value for the car...$5,307.33.

TOTAL COST FOR ONE YEAR   -0-

These are the advantages to starting a leasing corporation. When the year is over the stockholders can either keep the car or trade in on another or sell it outright. Either way, the cycle starts all over again; this time the present stockholders will be in a position to recommend you to other friends of theirs and enabling you to start more than one automobile leasing corporation. This year you can be driving a new Mercedes-Benz and your wife or your son or daughter can be driving a new Lincoln Continental.

*Mr. Jones, your credit card
application has just been approved!*

Carry All the Major Credit Cards You Want

I am going to take you through a series of steps to enable you to accumulate as many credit cards as you want: American Express, Diners, Carte Blanche, Master Charge, Visa, department store accounts, and even gas credit cards.

Regardless of whether you have ever had credit established or if your credit rating is bad, this plan will work for you. The objective of credit card companies is to give the cards to people who have proved to the credit bureau that they pay all of their bills on time.

When they receive an application for credit, they utilize a scoring method to check your qualifications. If you score high enough on the guide, they issue the card to you. It is just that simple. The following is the guide normally used in processing your application:

Years Employed

one year or less	0
one to three years	1
four to six years	3
seven to ten years	4

Your age

20 to 24	0
25 to 64	3
65 & over	0

Monthly Income

$100 to $500	1
$500 to $900	2
$900 to $1200	4
over $1200	6

Years at Same Address

6 months to 3 years	0
over five years	3

Occupation
Labor	1
Skilled (plumber)	3
Professional (CPA)	4

Your Monthly Bills
0 to $250	1
$250 and over	0

Credit History
Savings or loan this bank	5
Other bank loans	3
Savings & loan co.	3
Loan at finance co.	0

Home or Place of Residence
Renting	1
Own with mortgage	4
Own without mortgage	6
Living at home	0
Living with friends	0

Home Telephone
In name of applicant	3
No phone number	Decline

(If you don't show a home phone number, the loan will be turned down.)

Married or Single
Married	2
Single	0
Divorded	1

Dependents
one to three	1
over three	0
no dependents	0

Checking or Savings
Checking & savings	2
In your name, this bank	3

Years in area
one to three years	1
three to ten	3

Things to remember are: Have a phone in your name or one you can use on your application. You should have at least two years on the job. You should be earning over $150 per week.

Second Method

Whether a lender uses the scoring guide on your application or not, if you have a credit rating with a bank or a saving and loan, you are most likely to receive credit. Bank's loans are always considered hard to land, and if you have built your credit rating around banks, chances are you will have no problem.

How to Get the First Credit Card
1. Open a checking and saving account with three different banks (A.B.C.).
2. Borrow $250 from a friend.
3. Deposit the $250 in bank (A).
4. Wait four days and go into Bank (A) and ask for a loan of $250 offering to put up your savings account as collateral.
5. Go to bank (B) and deposit $250 you received from bank (A).
6. Wait four days and go to bank (B) and ask for a loan of $250 offering to put up your savings account as collateral.
7. Go to bank (C) and deposit the $250 in your savings account.
8. Wait four days and go to bank (C) and ask for a loan of $250 offering to put up your saving account as collateral.
9. Apply to two different charge accounts, one being a department store account and the other being a gas company. (Start out with small stores and small gas companies.)
10. In filling out your application, show only the three loans only after you have made at least one payment on each account and have waited at least four days for the payment to be processed.
11. Once you have received the credit cards from the department store and gas company, you should now start applying for other cards starting with other gas companies and other department stores, then moving up to Master Charge and Visa, completing the process with American Express and Diners. Remember that you must make at least $15,000 per year before you can acquire American Express.
12. You should charge at least one dollar on each credit card and pay it right away, preferably the same day — don't even wait for them to bill you. Just send in the payment with your name and address and credit card number. They will process it and it will show that you pay your bills ahead of time.
13. Now is the time to pay back your friend. Start out by paying off the loan at bank (C) and then retrace your steps backward until you are back at bank (A).

This method has not only brought you all the credit cards you want, but you have established credit with three banks. Don't hesitate, if you need a little extra money, go back to the banks and ask for a loan of $250 from each. This time, in all probability, you will be able to receive a signature loan. NO COLLATERAL.

"Come right in! Everything has been approved."

Open as Many Charge Accounts as You Desire

Most people would like to go into any store and buy a house full of furniture, a new TV, stereo system and even jewelry for your loved one on credit. With this chapter of Shortcuts to Becoming Rich, I am going to show you how this can be done.

One of the basic rules to remember is that the salesman and sales manager do not make one dime until your credit is approved and your purchase is processed, so keep that in mind when you start looking at new furniture. Ask the salesman for his help. Tell him that you would like to buy his beautiful bedroom set, but you don't know if you have established enough credit to buy it. He will be more than glad to help you.

If you have read the chapter entitled, "Carry All the Credit Cards You Want" and have followed the instructions in the chapter, you will have no problem in buying the furniture that you want on credit. If you haven't, here is an alternate plan.

Start out by going to a new homes subdivision in your area, you know, the ones that sell New Homes, not a real estate office that sells previously owned homes.

Make sure to pick out a subdivision you think is out of your income bracket. When you get there look around and tell the salesman that you want to buy one and you would like to fill out the papers and apply for the mortgage.

At this time he will have you fill out a preliminary credit application and sign a contract with a deposit. Here is how it works:

First: Sign the contract making sure that you read it.
Second: Tell the salesman that you did not bring your checkbook with you and you would like to sign a 30-day note for the deposit. He will be more than happy to oblige you.
Third: Tell him that you would rather fill the credit application at home where you have all your papers, and you will bring it to the mortgage company the following day.
Fourth: The following day, call the mortgage company and tell them you can't come by because you are going to be busy this week, and that you will be coming by early next week. Make sure you tell them your full name and the name of the subdivision. Make sure that you

	get the names of the person that you talked to at the mortgage company and the real estate salesman.
Fifth:	Now, you go into any store that you wish, and tell them that you are in the process of buying a new home and that you wish to establish credit with their store. Make sure when you fill out the credit application that you list the name of the mortgage company and who they can talk to as well as the name of the real estate company and who they are to talk to there. Chances are you will walk out of the store with the merchandise that same day. You can also fill out the credit application over the phone and save time.
Sixth:	After you have done this at several stores in town, call the real estate agent back and tell him that you have changed your mind and are not going to be able to buy the house because you have suddenly discovered that it is more than you can afford. If he gives you a hard time and will not let you out of the contract, all you do is fill out the credit report that goes to the mortgage company showing them your true picture and they will turn it down.

Warning notice: Our attorney cautions readers of this section to be aware of all laws regarding falsely written statements and/or false documents.

idea starters

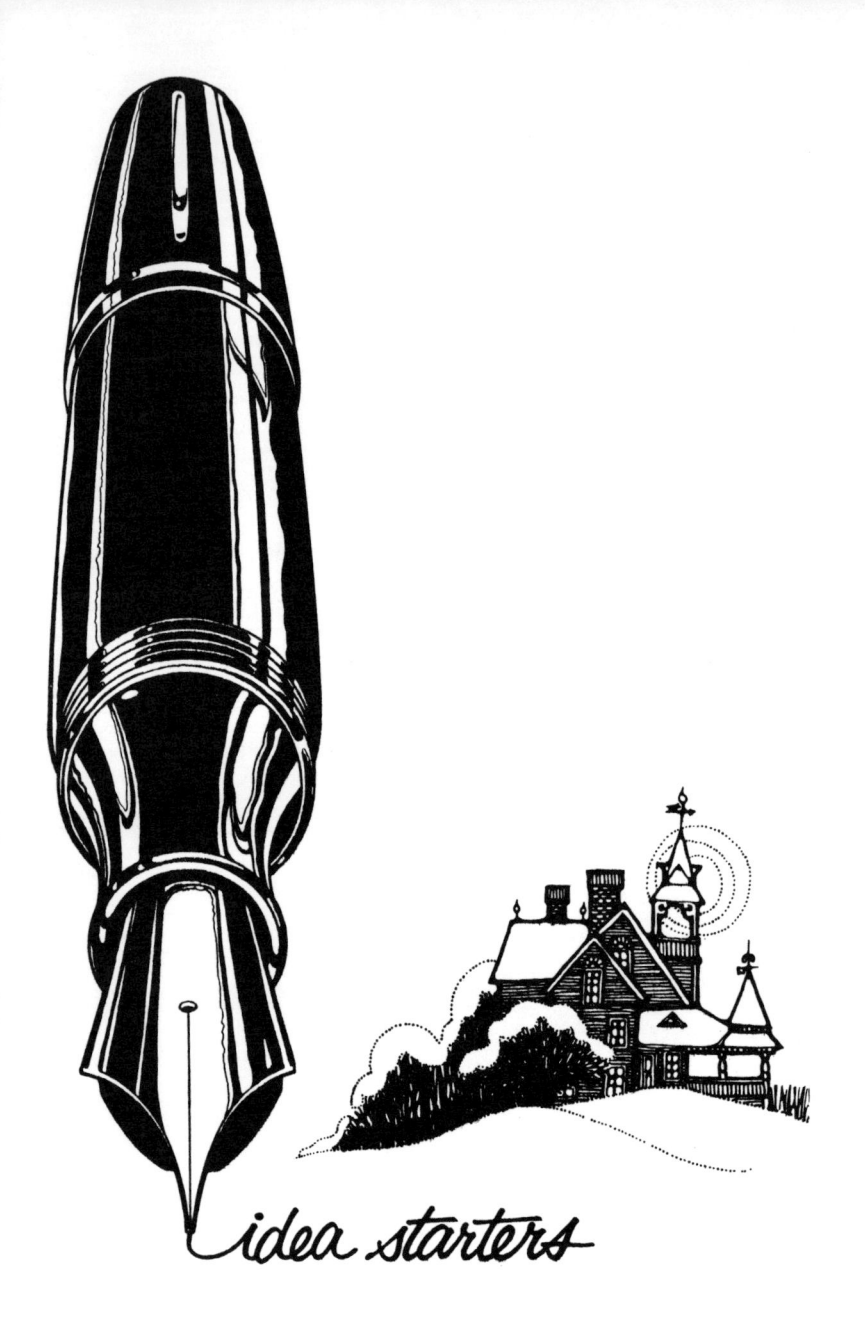

Live in a $100,000 Mansion of Your Choice

The easiest way to accomplish this is to offer your services as a house sitter. More and more real estate companies are looking for someone to house sit while their clients are on vacation. The very rich can't close down their houses when they go on vacation, like everyone else. They have servants and expenses that must go on. It sometimes takes years to find good servants, and if they close down the house for three or four months these people are out of a job.

It is a common practice these days for the rich to take off for four or five months or more during the year. But they have the problem of finding someone to house sit for the insurance companies will not insure a vacant house for more than thirty days.

All you do is compose a creative letter, offering your services as a house sitter. Walk down to the neighborhood printer and have about 100 copies xeroxed. Once you have the letter printed, then mail it to all the real estate companies in your area and sit back and wait for the offers to pour in.

In making up your letter, make sure you mention the fee you charge ($35 to $45 a month is fair), for you are not doing this to make money. The idea is to create the illusion of being rich while you are living in this mansion.

Offer references that can be verified and, if necessary, have yourself bonded for $100,000. This will erase any doubts they may have about having a stranger sitting in their house while they are on vacation.

Keep in mind that banks and savings and loan companies often have houses that are empty because of a death or repossessions. A house that sits empty for very long is a target for vandals. These organizations will be more than happy to interview you for the jobs.

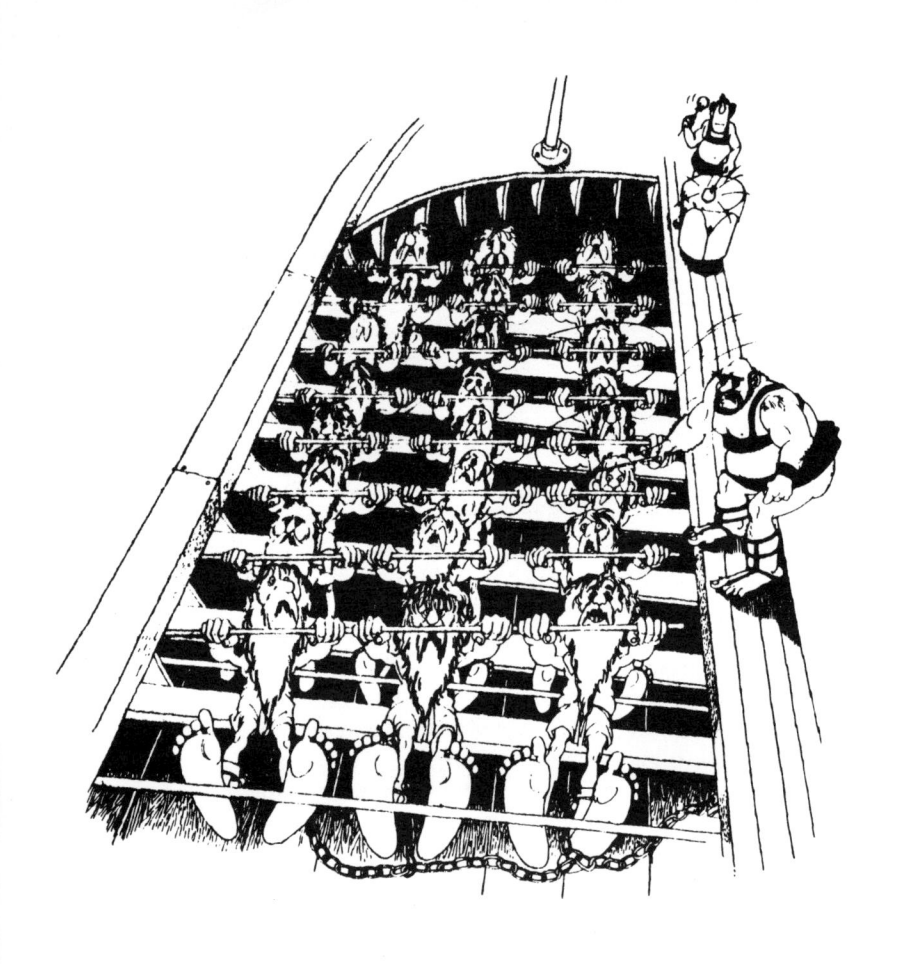

"Go from this to this!"

Have 10,000 People Selling Your Produc 60 Days

It is going to be nice to have 10,000 people selling your product in all the states in the next 60 days. And the best part is that it will cost you nothing in salaries. This is being done all over America right now by using jobbers, or as they were formerly known. "Specialty Salesmen". They are a large group of direct salesmen who sell products door to door, or by contacting various specialty stores that carry products ranging from office supplies, children's toys, business calculators to automobiles. It is estimated that there are about 750,000 men and women in the U.S. doing this form of selling today. And every day they are looking for new products to sell.

SOME OF THE COMPANIES THAT MAKE MILLIONS SELLING THEIR PRODUCTS BY USING THIS FORM OF SALESMAN ARE:
AMWAY DISTRIBUTORS   GIFTIME
FULLER BRUSH   SPECIALTY MERCHANDISE CORP.
NATIONAL PRESS   AVON
SUCCESS MOTIVATION   SHAKLEE CORPORATION

Here is a plan to get your share of this mammoth industry. The idea is to contact as many of these direct salesmen as possible. The easiest way to contact them is to place an ad in one or all of the following magazines:

Specialty Salesman Magazine
307 North Michigan Avenue
Chicago, IL 60601

Salesman's Opportunity
875 North Michigan Avenue
Chicago, IL 60611

Income Opportunities
380 Lexington Avenue
New York, NY 10017

Spare Time
8510 W. Oklahoma Avenue
Milwaukee, WI 53219

Send your letter to each magazine requesting a rate card and a free copy of their publication. Tell them in your letter that you are planning an advertising campaign for your product and that you feel that their publication will be a great assistance to your company.

My suggestion is that when you receive the free copies from the publishers, you study each ad that is advertising a product similar to yours. Cut out the ads so you can examine their format for selling their products. Check the size of the ad they are using (for you don't nt to spend more advertising dollars than is necessary.) Check the frequency of the ad (how many times they run per year), and finally the design of the ad (whether they use pictures of their products or just straight type). Remember if you only see the ad once, chances are they are not making a profit and it is a good idea to steer clear of their form of advertising.

Important: You must be able to run your ad at least three months in a row, so that you don't break the sequence. This is the only way that it will pay for you to advertise. Running an ad one month and then waiting for two months before you can get back in will lose credibility with the readers.

The cost of doing business this way is almost nil. The salesman will purchase your product at wholesale, read the instructions or selling tips you may include, and be on his way the following day pushing your product. (Make sure to have a big commission built in the retail price.) The more money the salesmen can make, the harder they will push your product.

The ideal way the jobbers like to operate is on a drop ship basis. This means that they will sell your product, give the customer a receipt and tell them that the product will be shipped to them in one week. In turn the jobber will deduct his commission and send you the balance for shipment of the product. In that way, he has no expenses for storing. If the jobber is able to operate on a drop ship basis, he does not have to tie up any money on inventory except for a sample kit.

If you would like full details on how drop shipping works, drop me a line in c/o Homeowners in Motion:

>	Elden Street
>	P.O. Box 607
>	Herndon, Virginia 22070.

I'll be glad to send you free information on how a method of drop-shipping is working for me. (Make sure to write Homeowners in Motion, *not* Northern Virginia Publishing Company.)

"OK, Mr. Smartmoney, we'll deposit $350,000 in your checking account this afternoon."

How to Get a $350,000 Line of Credit

The problem that most people face is that they have the desire and the ideas to make a fortune, but they don't have the capital to get started. It seems like once a person has found the money to put his plan into effect, he or she is an immediate success. So with this in mind, I am going to show you in detail how to raise a $350,000 line of credit. By the way, a line of credit is the same as having cash in the bank. The only difference is that the person (lending institution) lending you the money wants to know how the money is going to be spent before he transfers it to your checking account. So in essence you are able to borrow up to $350,000 at any time providing you can show how you are spending the money.

All you need is a good idea to make you rich. I am going to show you how to acquire the capital to put your plan into effect.

Have you ever heard the story that banks won't loan anyone money if they need it. Well, it's true. When you really need money, it is always the time when you get turned down. To solve that problem, you have to prove to them that you don't need the money. I know for I have been doing it for years, from a small $500 personal loan to a $500,000 business loan.

Turned down! Turned down! It seemed like it would never end until I decided to find out what the banks were looking for, and then to make sure that I provided them with information needed from that time on.

How to Acquire a New Auto Loan

Auto loans can sometimes be hard to get, especially if you have bad credit or if you have no credit established.

The only way to acquire a new auto loan if your credit is bad is to go out of the credit bureau area. Most credit bureaus have a radius of about 50 miles outside of a major city. In rural areas, the credit bureau sometimes takes in whole counties or sometimes two or three counties. The safest way is to establish credit in another credit bureau area. To do this you must set up a new residence (maybe at a friend's house), so that you will have a local address and phone number. Once you have established a new residence, go to a local bank and apply for a checking and saving account in your name only (if married, both names). Having a checking and saving account, apply for a $300 loan, telling the loan officer that your move to this area has cost more than you expected and you need a loan for 12 months to defray the moving expenses. Once you have the loan, make one payment as soon as possible — like the following week.

Two weeks after you have received the loan, you should apply for a new car loan, not at the bank but at the largest automobile dealership in the area, the one who sells the most cars per month. Just walk in and start looking for a new car. Once you have found a car that you like, sit down with the Finance and Insurance Respresentative in the dealership. (He is commonly called the F&I representative). Tell him that you just moved to the area and that you don't have much credit established.

Believe me, he will do everything possible for you to buy the car because his job depends on putting deals together. That's why the dealership sells the most cars. (The plan even works easier if you are buying a truck.)

This plan works almost 100% of the time. If for some reason it doesn't, try another dealer. I have talked to individuals who have worked this plan without setting up a new address, just going out of the credit bureau area. They have found it so easy that they were driving their new car the same day.

Having not established credit, it is almost as difficult to buy a new car as having bad credit, but not quite. The plan is a little easier, and much faster. All you have to do is go into any new car showroom and find the car you want, making sure it is within your budget, being sure again that the dealership is either largest or next to the largest in the area where you live. Having found the car that you want, sit down with the F&I representative and explain to him that you have not established any credit.

Now is the time to prove to him that you are an honest person who will make all the payments on time, and that you need the car to keep the new job that you hve. Be sincere!

In most cases you will be driving out that afternoon, because of two reasons. Again, it is the job of the F&I representative to put ideals together, so the dealership will still be number one in the area. Second, most of the dealerships that are holding the title of being number one are signing behind you. What this means is that if the bank doesn't think you are strong enough financially on your own, they will ask the dealership to sign their name as a co-signer for your loan. You may think that this is out of the question, since the dealer does not know you from Adam. Well, let me tell you that this has been going on in dealerships across the country for years. For as difficult as it may seem to you, the dealer has about 2% repossessions a year. And even if they do, who is in a better position to resell the car than the dealer, Besides, if he doesn't sell you a car he doesn't make any money.

In one case, a dealer sold a new truck to a young man 21 years of age, who didn't even have a job and still lived with his parents. This particular dealer even went to the trouble of finding him a job so the sale of the new truck could go through. So if you need a new car, buy one today with this method.

A $350,000 Line of Credit

Acquiring a $350,000 line of credit is not child's play; it is hard work and sometimes downright frustrating. But if you plan to be successful in life you must resort to hard work and planning. For if you don't have a brother who owns a bank, where else can you turn but to yourself.

Over the years, I have found that if you want lending institutions to lend you money, you must prove to them that you have a plan and that you will stick to your plan, come hell or high water. For no one wants to lend money to a person who, at the first sight of what seems to be an insurmountable problem, takes off running, leaving the bank holding the proverbial empty bag.

When I say that you need a plan, I mean a "Detailed Plan" from start to finish, leaving nothing to chance, having all the objections that will be raised (as to why they shouldn't lend you the money) answered.

What you are planning to do with the money, I have no way of knowing. But I must assume that you are planning to start a business of some sort, not running off to the Caribbean until the money runs out. So with this assumption we will start.

First, I want to point out to you that I have found that starting a business or a coporation from scratch has always been the most profitable in the long run but not by buying someone else's business (headaches), for if they were making money they probably would not be selling. This is true and always will be true. The only exception I have found to this fact is that when a man is so wealthy that he just doesn't have time to run the business and make it profitable any longer, he then might be willing to sell. But most men who are really wealthy have not become that way by giving up anything that is making a profit. Even if they have to hire someone to run it and take a smaller profit in doing so, they will hold on to it until it is showing a deficit, and then and only then will make an attempt to sell.

I will show you how to borrow large sums of money by showing you an example and a step-by-step method of how others have been successful in the past in securing large loans with local banks and with other lending institutions.

Keeping in mind that these lending institutions are here to lend money, not to turn you down, it is your job to prove to them that you are a secure, hard working individual who will guard their money as though it were your own, and make it profitable.

How to Establish a $350,000 Line of Credit by Creating Your Own Money Making Business

This is a story of a man with imagination and a burning desire to have his own office building and a $50,000 a year income. Owning a building, like few other businesses, can bring you a large income and a tremendous line of credit for the rest of your life.

Twenty-five years ago, a department store expanded its business by building a new 150,000 square foot building. Fifteen years later the business folded, because of the untimely death of the owner. The executor of the estate sold the building for $200,000 to a local investor. The new owner tried to do something with the building for about six months before giving up. He just couldn't find someone (corporation), to lease the 150,000 square foot department store. When the young man with the burning desire came by and suggested that he would like to lease the building for 99 years, the owner was very interested. The young man was new at managing a building and for that matter, had no experience in the investment field whatsoever. But the owner was sitting with a vacant building on his hands and no way to retrieve his $200,000. Since both of them were anxious they soon came to an agreement and settled on the property thirty days later. The young man made an offer to pay $36,000 for the annual rental for the first 20 years, and to pay $26,000 a year for the balance of the 99-year lease.

It turned out to be a fantastic deal for both of them, for the leasee went to the bank with the new lease in hand and borrowed $200,000 that he had originally paid for the building agreesing to pay it back over 10 years at $25,000 a year including interest. This gave him an income of $16,000 a year for the next 10 years and $36,000 a year for the balance of the 20 years, plus having his bank loan paid for by the lew leassee.

Now let's see what the young man with all the imagination did with the building. After weeks of trying to find tenants in the normal fashion, he hit on something that no one else in his area had tried.

He prepared an article for the local newspaper offering the office space for the unheard of low price of $1.25 per square foot. This price was far less than the prevailing price of $6.00 a square foot for similar offices in the same area. The article appeared in the classified section under "OFFICE SPACE FOR RENT." The ad read as follows:

OFFICE SPACE FOR RENT
$1.25 Sq. Ft.
Build to Suit... within reason
Call John Shumway   441-5678

The newspaper campaign brought a landslide of responses from all over the city: Lawyers starting a new practice, insurance agents, small publishing companies, florists, a printing company, real estate brokers, etc., etc., all who had been working either out of their homes or sharing offices with other small companies. Nine months later the newly created office building was completely 100 percent occupied. The rent, after taking 30,000 square feet for new wash rooms, storage and management, was $150,000.

After the young man had the new tenants signed on a lease, he went to a savings and loan armed with $150,000 of secured rental agreements and arranged for a $75,000 mortgage to make the improvements he had promised the new tenants.

Here is the financial picture he presented the Savings and Loan.

Cost

Cost for 99-year lease	$000,000
Improvements to building	75,000
A. New wash rooms	$18,000
B. New air conditioner	24,000
C. Partitions for offices	26,000
D. Storage rooms & management offices	7,000

Income

120,000 square feet leased at $1.25 (10 years)	$150,000

Expenses

Light	$ 6,000
Heat	4,000
Real Estate Taxes	15,000
Repairs	7,000
99-year lease payments (annually)	36,000
Miscellaneous	3,000
Janitor Services	10,000
Management	15,000
Payments on building improvement loan	8,000
TOTAL	**$104,000**
INCOME TO YOUNG MAN WITH IMAGINATION	$ 46,000

The loan officer had no problems justifying the loan to the Board of Directors of the Saving and Loan, and the young man with

$75,000 in hand proceeded to improve the building to the specifications of his newly acquired tenants.

At this point you may say, "What does this story have to do with securing a $350,000 line of credit from a bank or a Savings and Loan? Well, I'll tell you. The young man will have no problem in securing a loan up to $450,000 if he wanted to start another project, for he has what the banks are looking for: A sincere interest in guarding their money, creativeness, a desire to work hard and, last but not least, a burning desire to make the deal work no matter what it takes.

Here is a list of things to be covered in presenting a proposal to loan officers:

1. How much money is required to purchase or to lease;
2. What exactly is the money going to be used for (in detail);
3. How will repayment to made and from what source (rents, manufacturing);
4. How much experience and what are your qualifications;
5. How will the lenders' money be protected (collateral);
6. What precautions have you taken in case you are sick or unable to complete the project. (Insurance is sometimes the answer.)

Pyramiding

Here is another way to borrow large sums of money almost overnight. The plan is called pyramiding.

Go to any local bank and borrow $5,000 and place it in another bank in a saving account, explaining to the loan officer that you wish to use the deposit as a compensating balance for a loan of $25,000. Most federal banks have a plan by which you can borrow five times your compensating balance, provided you have a detailed plan of how the money is to be used, then you can go to another bank and deposit the $25,000 as a compensating balance following the same plan. This plan sometimes requires the use of several banks when large sums of money are loaned.

Here is a partial list of companies offering venture capital. These lending institutions will finance unsecured ventures that a lot of conventional banks and savings and loans wouldn't touch with a ten-foot pole. If it is an honest straight business transaction, they will consider it. Give them a try. You will be surprised at the information you can learn and the progress you will make in the accomplishment of your particular line of credit goal.

Bea Associates, Inc.
366 Madison Ave.
New York, NY 10017

Alison Promotions
5834 Soledad Mt. Rd.
La Jolla, CA 92307

Cambridge Banking Partners
1711 Security Life Bldg.
Denver, CO 80202

David Morgenthaler
1033 National City Bank Bldg.
Cleveland, OH 44114

Financial Consultants
Box 297
Uniontown, KY 42461

General Pacific Investments
321 10th St.
San Francisco, CA 94103

Hanover Small Business
Investment, Box 747
Charlotte, NC 28231

International Capital Corp.
800 Dorchester W.
Montreal 113, Que, Canada

Mid Tex Capital Corp.
104 North Ave. E.
Clifton, TX 76634

National Lead Company
111 Broadway
New York, NY 10006

Loeb, Rhodes and Company
42 Wall St.
New York, NY 10005

Professional SBIC
5979 W. 3rd St.
Los Angeles, CA 90036

Research Industries, Inc.
123 N. Pitt St., Suite A201
Alexandria, VA

Rockefeller Brothers, Inc.
30 Rockefeller Plaza
New York, NY 10020

Standard Growth Capital
Box 10106
Knoxville, TN 37919

Sun Capital Corporation
Box 10809
Pittsburgh, PA 15236

Catawba Capital Corp.
Box 3121
Charlotte, NC 28203

Developers Equity Corp.
9348 Santa Monica Blvd.
Beverly Hills, CA 90210

Explorer Fund, Inc.
28 State St.
Boston, MA 02109

Financial Resources, Inc.
1909 Storick Bldg.
Memphis, TN 38103

Intercon Investment Co.
100 S. Wacker Dr.
Chicago, IL 60606

Investment Funds, Inc.
5513 Princess Anne Rd.
Virginia Beach, VA 23462

Montag and Caldwell, Inc.
2901 1st National Bank Tower
Atlanta, GA 30303

North Star Industries
4570 W. 77th St.
Minneapolis, MN 55435

Pan American Capital Corp.
24 Commerce St.
Newark, NJ 07102

R. and D. Capital Co.
2700 Merced St.
San Leandro, CA 94577

Resources and Tech, Mgt. Co.
Box 100
Chestnut Hill, MA 02167

Russ and Company
Alamo National Building
San Antonio, TX 78205

State Street Bank Company
225 Franklin St.
Boston, MA 02101

Tait and Legge
110 Allens Creek Rd.
Rochester, NY 14618

Technology Search Associates
1 Spruce Hill Rd.
Weston, MA 02193

U.A.G. Investment Corp.
Box 67
Robesonia, PA 19551

Vanguard Venture Capital
301 E. Main St.
Barrington, IL 60010

Venture Capital Corp.
2540 Frontage Rd.
Northfield, IL 60093

Western Group, Inc.
Box 1273
Weston, CT 06880

William Blair and Company
135 S. LaSalle St.
Chicago, IL 60603

Wilshire Capital Corp.
10000 Santa Monica Blvd.
Los Angeles, CA 90067

Venture Capital Corp.
540 Frontage Rd.
Northfield, IL 60093

Sample Forms to be Used
In presenting your Proposal to the Banks

1. APPLICANT _____ PHONE _____
2. ADDRESS _____
3. AUTHORIZED OFFICER _____
4. ADDRESS _____ PHONE _____
5. PURPOSE OF LOAN _____
6. AMOUNT REQUESTED _____ TERM _____
7. SECURITY TO BE PLEDGED _____ 1ST ( ) 2ND ( ) OTHER ( )
8. LOCATIONS OF SECURITY _____
9. APPRAISED OR FACE VALUE OF SECURITY _____
10. ASSETS_____
11. LIABILITIES _____
12. NET PROFIT OR NET LOSS LAST 5 YEARS (show loss figures in parentheses)

13. NET WORTH LAST 5 YEARS

LOAN PACKAGE SHOULD HAVE DOCUMENTS LISTED BELOW.
INCLUDE AS MANY AS POSSIBLE ON PROJECT.

14. ( ) LEASE COPIES
15. ( ) MAPS
16. ( ) PICTURES
17. ( ) M.A.I. APPRAISAL
18. ( ) BALANCE SHEET
19. ( ) PROFIT & LOSS STATEMENTS
20. ( ) HISTORICAL BACKGROUND
21. ( ) PLAT
22. ( ) SPECIFICATIONS

23. ( ) DEEDS
24. ( ) CREDIT REPORTS
25. ( ) FINANCIAL STATEMENTS
26. ( ) IMPROVEMENT BIDS
27. ( ) EXISTING MORTGAGE
        VERIFICATIONS
28. ( ) ITEMIZED COST & VALUE
        LIST
29. ( ) OTHER _____
30. ( ) OTHER _____

REMARKS _____

Sample Form to be Used
In Presenting your Proposal to the Banks

VALUE OF SECURITY OFFERED:

LAND: Cost $ _____ or appraisal $ _____

#Square Feet _____ Date bought, optioned, or escrowed _____

Improvements: Cost $ _____ or appraisal $ _____

Total Value: Cost $ _____ and appraisal $ _____

Details: (*Important* to answer all applicable questions)

LAND DEVELOPMENT.   Water _____ Sewer _____

Roads _____ Utilities _____

Other _____

Building: Type of Construction _____

#of Buildings _____ #of Stories _____ Total Sq. Ft. _____

#of Units _____ Rent per Unit _____ Debt per Unit _____

#of Rooms _____ Rent per Room _____ Debt per Room _____

#of Studios _____ @ $_____ Sq. Ft. _____

#1 BR _____ @ $_____ Sq. Ft. _____

#2 BR _____ @ $_____ Sq. Ft. _____

Other _____

Air Cond. _____ Elevators _____ Parking _____ Pool _____

Other _____

ABILITY OF PROJECT TO REPAY: (Attach statements of income/expenses)

Gross Income $ _____
_____ % of Vacancy $ _____
Expenses $ _____
0Net Available for Debt Service $ _____

Debt X Income: $ _____

32

"OK, we have all agreed to go along with your plan."

How to Stop Your Creditors

Do you feel that you have yourself so far in debt that you can go no further? ... You have sold everything that you have to sell, and have borrowed from every friend you know. Are your monthly bills more than your monthly paycheck? Well, don't feel desperate any longer. This part of the book will show you how to come out of debt, and will give financial freedom once again.

The rarely used Federal Bankruptcy Law is called Chapter 13. I know that you have probably never heard of this law, for fortunately too few attorneys fail to tell their clients about it. It is one of the laws put on the books for the little guy. The person who can't afford to pay the high cost of bankruptcy or, for that matter, does not want to go bankrupt against his creditors. All he wants to do is pay his bills and have a little left over each month for himself.

The Wage Earners Plan or Chapter 13 as it is called, gives the debtor a chance to pay the bills of his creditors without filing bankruptcy in the normal manner. There is only one requirement for the individual to be eligible under the Wage Earners Act. The debtor must be a person whose principal income is derived from salary or commission. It does not matter whether or not an idividual earns $600 or $600,000 a year, everyone is eligible as long as he or she is employed.

The debtor works out a plan suitable to his income and brings the plan to the court, wherein the debtor agrees to pay off his debts in full within a period not to exceed three years. The court decides if this plan is workable on both sides. If the majority of creditors agree to accept the plan, it is then approved by the court which appoints a trustee, who is entrusted to make your payments to the creditors.

This procedure may sound complicated, but it is far from being complex. It was designed and constructed to keep the debtor from creditor harassment, and protect him from law suits. Even if the law suits have begun, Chapter 13 will stop them cold. Sit down and list all your bills and your monthly income, then deduct all your monthly expenses (food, gas for your car, rent, other). The amount left over should be close to the amount you would want to use for paying your bills.

In no way am I offering any legal advice. I am, however, trying to bring to your attention certain Federal Government laws, which were designed to help the little guy, especially when he is down and there does not seem to be any other way out for him.

If you believe that Chapter 13 is for you, then I advise you to hire an attorney who is recommended by a friend or maybe someone you work with. Consult with him. He will give you his alternatives, and he will help you find the best way to overcome your dilemma. Filing under Chapter 13 hardly takes any legal fees, so you should shop around and try to find a reasonable fee. Not all attorneys have the same fee for this service.

I don't want to be redundant, but many lawyers will want you to file bankruptcy rather than file under the Wage Earner's Act, because there are more fees in bankruptcy than Chapter 13 petition. So another solution to this problem is to start making a few phone calls. Now that lawyers can advertise, I think you will find some of their secretaries will have the schedule for the fees right at their desk. Although there is no requirement that you engage an attorney to file your petition, I believe that if you find one who is knowledgeable and is not trying to get you to pay his next payment on his yacht, that with his help, filing your petition will be a lot easier.

The forms to be used for filing under Chapter 13 may be found in the Federal District Clerk's office, or your attorney should have them on hand. I am attaching samples so you may be familiar with them.

The Federal District Court's filing costs vary between $20 and $35 paid usually at the time of filing. Any time during the three year time limit, the court can reduce or suspend payments from the debtor because of illness, loss of work, or strikes. Remember it is based on your income, so if your income is less than when you filed, it can be adjusted.

SCHEDULE A

STATEMENT OF ALL DEBTS
CREDITORS TO WHOM PRIORITY IS SECURED BY THE ACT

TAXES: Amount due or claime

United States . . . . $ _____
State of . . . . $ _____
Other . . . . $ _____

OTHER CREDITORS
Except as specifically noted, the debtor is unable to state whether or not the creditors listed below have valid liens upon property of the estate.

Name of Creditor and Address	Monthly Payment Due under the Contract	Total Amount Due or Claimed	Is the Debt Disputed
(Be sure to Use Complete Address of Creditor)			

SCHEDULE B
STATEMENT OF ALL PROPERTY

1. Real Estate _____(Equity Value)$ _____
2. Household goods _____(Resale Value)$ _____
3. Automobile _____(Resale Value)$ _____
3a. Deposits of money in bank and elsewhere
5. Property in reversion, remainder, expectancy, trusts, patents, copyrights, trademarks, shares in shipping vessels, books, prints, horses and other animals, debts due on open account, negotiable instruments and securities, cash surrender value of insurance, and unliquidated claims _____$ _____
6. Other personal property _____$ _____
   Total _____$ _____

PROPERTY CLAIMED AS EXEMPT FROM THE OPERATION OF THE ACT OF CONGRESS RELATING TO BANKRUPTCY

For the purposes of this Chapter XIII proceeding only, all personal property exemptions are waived.

STATEMENT OF AFFAIRS AND EXECUTORY CONTRACTS

1. Other residences during past six years:
   (a) _____From_____To _____
   (b) _____From_____To _____
   (c) _____From_____To _____
2. Have you, within the six years immediately preceeding the filing of this Petition:
   (a) Been in partnership with anyone or engaged in any business? Yes _____ No _____
   (b) Been proceeded against under the Bankruptcy Act? Yes _____ No _____
3. Have you, within two years immediately prior to the filing of the original petition herein:
   (a) Kept books of account, or received income from any source other than for wages or for hire?
       Yes _____ No _____ If so, state _____
   (b) Maintained any bank account or safe deposit boxes in your own name or with others?
       Yes _____ No _____ If so, state _____
   (c) Made any assignment for the benefit of or a general settlement with creditors? Yes _____
       No _____ If so, state _____
4. Have you within one year prior to the filing of the original petition herein:
   (a) Transferred or disposed of any property or suffered any loss from fire, theft or gambling?
       Yes _____ No _____ If so, state _____
   (b) Been a party-plaintiff or defendant to any suit? Yes _____ No _____
       If so, state _____
5. Have any executions or attachments been levied against your property within the four months immediately preceeding the filing of the original petition herein? Yes _____ No _____
   If so, state _____
6. Where and when did you file your last Federal and State income tax return? _____
7. Do you hold any property in trust for any other person? Yes _____ No _____
   If so, state _____
8. Are you a party to any executory contracts? Yes _____ No _____
   If so, state _____

_____
Debtor

IN THE DISTRICT COURT OF THE UNITED STATES
FOR THE

IN THE MATTER OF

In proceedings for a Wage
Earner Plan under Chapter
XIII.

_____, DEBTOR

No. _____

DEBTOR'S PLAN

The above named debtor proposes under Chapter XIII of the Bankruptcy Act, more especially Section 646 thereof, the following plan:

The debts of the debtor, duly proved and allowed, shall be paid to the holders thereof in full accordance with the provisions of the Bankruptcy Act and this plan.

The debtor, or his employer, shall pay to the Trustee out of his future earnings and wages the sum of $_____ each _____. The Trustee shall make distribution of the funds so received by paying: (1) The filing fee; (2) the fees and costs required by provisions of Section 659 of the Act; and (3) the creditors.

Secured debts held by creditors who accept the plan shall have priority over the unsecured debts and shall be paid prorata except:

The unsecured debts shall be dealt with generally and paid prorate; provided, that where the amount or balance of any unsecured debt is less than $10.00 it may be paid in full.

This plan is proposed to provide a schedule of payment which does not materially or adversely affect the interest of any creditor whose claim is secured by a lien upon the property of the debtor. The claim of any secured creditor whose interest may be materially or adversely affected hereby shall not be dealt with by this plan until such as that creditor may file with the Court its written acceptance.

The future earnings and wages of the debtor are submitted to the supervision and control of the court for the purpose of enforcing the plan.

Title to the property of the debtor shall revest in the debtor upon the completion of the payments provided for by this plan or upon the dismissal of these proceedings unless upon such dismissal the debtor consents to adjudication as a bankrupt.

The court may from time to time during the period of extension increase or reduce the amount of any of the installment payments provided by the plan, or extend or shorten the time for any such payments, where it shall be made to appear, after hearing upon notice to the debtor and the trustee, that the circumstances of the debtor so warrant or require; provided, that nothing in this plan shall be construed to prevent the granting of a discharge to the debtor as provided by Section 661 of the Act.

The debtor further represents that he is able to carry out his plan and submits the following:

DEBTOR'S BUDGET

Employer: _____ Occupation: _____
Length of service with present employer: _____ No. of Dependents: _____

MONTHLY EXPENSES	MONTHLY INCOME
Rent or house payment......... $ _____	Take-Home Pay of Debtor ..... $ _____
Utilities..................... $ _____	Take-Home Pay of Spouse ..... $ _____
Groceries .... $ _____	Other Income .... $ _____
Clothing.................... $ _____	
Transportation .... $ _____	TOTAL MONTHLY INCOME $ _____
Insurance................... $ _____	Less Expenses and Payments.... $ _____
Miscellaneous .... $ _____	Excess...................... $ _____
Total Expenses .... $ _____	
Payments proposed under	
the plan .... $ _____	
TOTAL EXPENSES	
AND PAYMENTS.......... $ _____	

IN THE DISTRICT COURT OF THE UNITED STATES
FOR THE

IN THE MATTER OF

In proceedings for a Wage
Earner Plan under Chapter
XIII.

_____, DEBTOR   No. _____

APPLICATION FOR PERMISSION TO FILE PETITION UNDER
CHAPTER XIII WITHOUT DEPOSIT OF COSTS AND
FOR APPOINTMENT OF TRUSTEE

_____ S.S. No. _____, the above named debtor, respectfully represents:

1. That your petitioner herein is a citizen of the United States, without money or means and cannot obtain the money with which to pay the necessary fees for the filing of this petition.

2. That the petitioner has filed herewith a petition under Chapter XIII of the Act of Congress relating to Bankruptcy and a Plan proposing to effect an extension of time to pay debts out of future earnings and praying that proceedings be had upon the petition in accordance with the provisions of Chapter XIII of said Act; that by the Plan, all future earnings and wages are submitted to the supervision and control of the Court for the purpose of consummating the Plan.

3. That your Petitioner is regularly employed by _____

4. That the appointment of a Trustee to take charge of the earnings and wages of your petitioner in accordance with the Plan referred to above is necessary to preserve the estate of your petitioner and to prevent loss thereto, and to insure the payment of the necessary costs and fees, and that the employer named above should be ordered to deduct from the wages of your petitioner the sum proposed in the Plan and pay such sum forthwith to the Trustee appointed by this Court until such time as the Plan submitted by your Petitioner is confirmed or until the further order of this Court.

WHEREFORE, your petioner prays for permission on the part of this Court to file the petition under Chapter XIII of the Bankruptcy Act without the deposit of fees required by law at the time of the filing of the petition, and that a Trustee be appointed forthwith to take charge of the earnings and wages of your petitioner; that your petitioner's employer described above to be ordered to deduct the amount of the payments proposed by the Plan from the earnings and wages of your petitioner and pay the said sum forthwith to such Trustee until such time as the Plan submitted by your petitioner is confirmed or until further order of this Court and for such other relief as the Court deems just and proper.

_____
Debtor

STATE OF _____
                                    ss.
COUNTY OF _____

I, a Debtor in the within described proceedings, who subscribed to the foregoing document, do hereby make solemn oath that the statements contained therein and in the attached documents are true and complete according to the best of my knowledge, information and belief.

_____
Debtor

Subscribed and sworn to before me this _____ day of _____, 19 __
My Commission Expires:

_____   _____
                                                         Notary Public

Subscribed and sworn to before me, a notary public in and for the county and state aforesaid, this _____ day of _____, 19 _____ .

Term expires: _____
                                                         Notary Public

_____

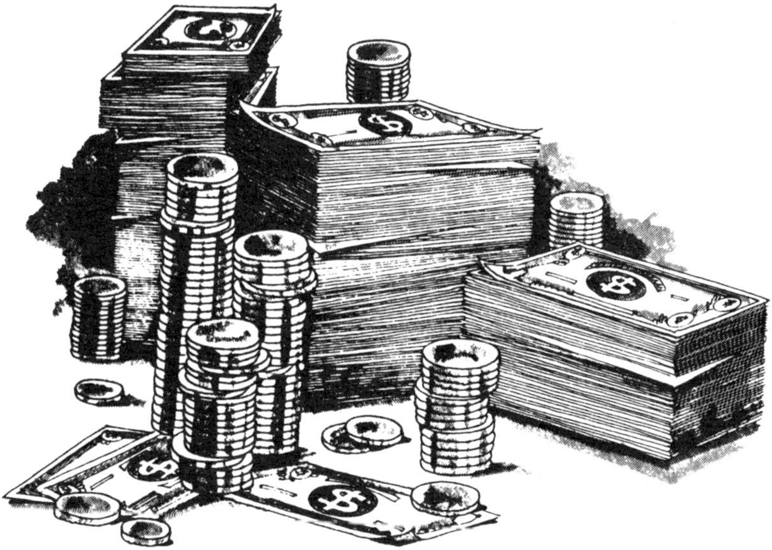

Are You the Missing Heir to $12 Million Dollars

You or someone you know may be entitled to share in a lost estate, Missing Heirs International, for the past thirty-five years, have been finding owners for an estimated twenty billion dollars worth of unclaimed property. This fabulous and little-known treasure is made up of unclaimed or forgotten estates, savings deposits, stocks and dividends, utility deposits, government bonds, checks and postal savings.

Although millions of dollars have been found for eighty-thousand people, the majority of unclaimed dollars grows every year by at least another billion dollars. This unclaimed money has attracted the attention of every state government. They have introduced into law ways of taking over the money from banks, courts, insurance companies and corporations that have been holding it. Most state governments take the money and hold it for eventual claimers. But some states take over the money permanently under the right of escheat, which means that the state is acting like the Lords of yesterday who took over all unclaimed estates for themselves.

Millions of people could claim their inheritance, if they only knew they were heirs and if they could be found. It is for sure that most state governments aren't very anxious to find the missing claimants to his or her lost estate.

Why are there so many missing heirs and so much unclaimed money? To begin with, there is NO central, national registration of all unclaimed or abandoned sums. Here are some other factors too. We live in a fast moving country. Millions of families change residence every year. Many fail to leave accurate mailing addresses; some fail to leave any. Most of us do, but the post office only retains such records for two years.

In any case, that money ought to be in your pocket right now. You could be spending it, investing it, living in luxury. It's yours. Missing Heirs International makes a living by bringing unclaimed money and rightful owners together. They work locating an unclaimed sum and tracking down the heirs. In return, the heirs give Missing Heirs International a percentage of what they get.

In order to find out if you are one of the lucky ones who is an heir to a fortune, write:

>Bantam Books, Inc.
>414 East Golf Rd.
>Des Plaines, IL 60016

Send $2.30 and ask for the book entitled, IS THERE A FOR-TUNE WAITING FOR YOU?

This book lists thousands of missing heirs and their former addresses. Also included are forms on how to file for missing fortunes.

Due to the nature of the book, the author has advised that the public, which has shown an interest in the subject of missing heirs, write the author requesting a search of his index and inquiring whether or not he will find money for them. The author requests that in order to answer all the letters, the following must be met:

1. Write only a very short letter.
2. Enclose a self-addressed, stamped envelope for reply.
3. *DO NOT* send it certified or registered mail. It will be refused by the author.

Should you wish to communicate with the author, write:

Mr. Theodore W. Roth
Missing Heirs International
11 West 42nd Street
New York, NY 10036

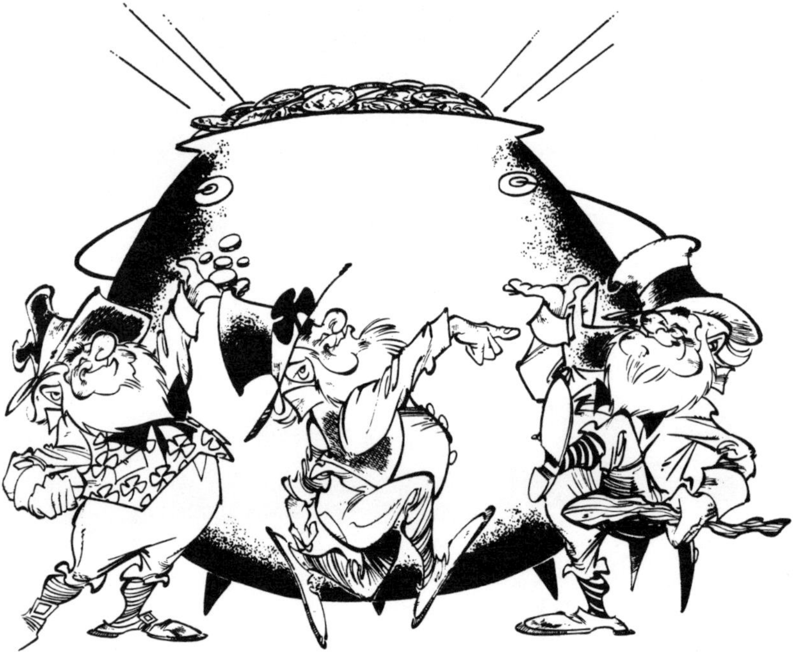

How to Spend $20 and Make $150 a Week

Spend $20 and become a Notary Public in your home state.

Every state has almost the same procedures to become a Notary Public. All you do is write or call the capitol of your state, and ask whoever answers who you should talk to about being a notary. There are only a few requirements that you must meet. The greatest advantage is that you can operate right out of your home. You must be of good moral character; you must be over 21 years of age; and you must swear that you will execute the office of Notary Public to the best of your ability.

Bond

Some state require that you be bonded for $1,000. In order to satisfy the requirement, just call an insurance company and they will send you the forms. It will probably cost about $15 to be bonded for one year. Some states take a guarantee that you are a forthright, upstanding citizen in your community from two residents who have lived in the state for over two years in lieu of posting a bond.

Starting Your Notary Public Business

You will probably make about $150 per week as a Notary Public, if you follow a few simple instructions:

First: Contact a sign maker and tell him that you would like a sign made up stating your name, phone, that you are a Notary Public, and the hours that you are open.

Note the example on the following page:

```
NOTARY PUBLIC

Mary Smith

Phone:  256-4466

Hours:  8:00 AM to 6:00 PM

7 Days a Week
```

Hang the sign outside your home so it can be seen by passing traffic.

Second: Contact as many people in your community as you can

telling them you are a Notary Public and the hours you will be open. You can also state that you will open any hour of the night for an extra fee.

The best method is to have a letter drawn up and run off on a printed form (about 100 copies). It should cost you no more than $5. Then mail the letters to all of the local retailers in your area: drug stores, grocery stores, automobile dealers, clothing stores, etc. You won't need envelopes, for you fold the letter three times and staple it closed. Then you address the outside of it. Try to use bulk mailing if you can, or ask the post office for the least expensive way to mail them.

You will probably find that once the word gets around that you are a Notary Public and are able to notarize forms, you will build up quite a following.

The state usually allows you to charge 50¢ to $1 per form, and a special fee if you are inconvenienced.

Note the example of a letter for mailing

NOTARY PUBLIC

Mary Jones
16 S.E. 15th Street
Fort Lauderdale, FL 33316
Phone: 256-4466

Dear Sir:

    I would like to inform you that I am a Notary Public licensed by the state of Florida.

    I am 76 years of age, and this is my only form of income. I will greatly appreciate any business that you are able to send me.

Sincerely,

Mary Jones,
Notary Public
for the state of Florida

OFFICE HOURS: 8:00 AM to 6:00 PM
7 Days a Week
Special fee of $2 for business after office hours.
Please call first. Thank you.

FOR SALE BY OWNER
Distributor Sales Kit

Homeowners InMotion®

One Homeowners Plaza, Box 607
Herndon, Virginia 22070

"3,000 Distributors Now in Operation"

How to Start Your Own Real Estate Company

Dear Real Estate Tycoon:

I know this is an unusual way to open this chapter, i.e. calling you REAL ESTATE TYCOON!

But this is going to be a Unique chapter about Real Estate's newest opportunity.

I live in Herndon, Virginia (just outside of the Nation's capital) and also own a home in Fort Lauderdale, Florida, and I have hit on something big, I mean BIG! It took me from a meager position as a clerk in a Real Estate office (take home pay about $85 a week) to owning my own Real Estate company. All of this because of a new IDEA, which we think is the greatest innovation in the Real Estate business since sliced bread.

This is no joke and in the next five minutes I will prove it to you. That you, too, can make $1000 per week, or perhaps even more, since the only limit is your own initiative...

The name of the company is HOMEOWNERS IN MOTION, and the IDEA behind the company is that we offer a complete Sales Kit which enables the homeowner to sell his home without a broker.

Whether it's a house, condominium, farm, business, or vacation home, you will profit by helping people help themselves.

You probably know that if a homeowner uses the services of a licensed Real Estate Broker, he is required by law to pay a commission when the house is sold (usually between 4% to 7%). A 6% commission on a $45,000 house is $2,700.00. That's a hefty chunk. But you can help them keep that money and sell their house faster by using HOMEOWNERS IN MOTION Sales Kit.

Your first question is why am I willing to share this IDEA, knowing first hand how powerful it is. The answer is simple. Since the market potential is too vast for me to handle alone, the next step would be to establish HOMEOWNERS IN MOTION distributorships and give them the full benefit of my idea and experience. The profits are exceptionaly high and we dro-ship the sales kits to your customers directly.

We've set everything up for you in a Custom Ready to Sell Package, including *mailers, advertising,* and even a sample "HOMEOWNERS IN MOTION" SALES KIT which provides every item and piece of information from pricing to settlement.

We provide everything so you can get started quickly... if you start now. The saying, "He who hesitates is lost," has never been more applicable. Please start moving on a proven winner while it's HOT! Your recognition of the potential of this selling innovation, coupled with the valuable information we will provide you is your ticket to success.

Do you get the idea that we believe in this...BIG? Well, you're right. After five weeks, I quit my full-time position as clerk because HOMEOWNERS IN MOTION had developed more business than I could handle.

I started out with a mailing of 25 letters and then, by word of mouth and a small ad in a local newspaper, more and more orders poured in for the "HOMEOWNERS IN MOTION" SALES KIT. I realized a net profit of $504.00 in the first week on the sale of 21 kits; second week — 34 kits; and, in the third week — 61 kits. I just couldn't believe the staggering multiplication.

My special thanks go to you for taking the time to read about one of my ideas, and the newest Real Estate opportunity in the country. Send for your "HOMEOWNERS IN MOTION" SALES KIT. Today!! Next week or next month may be too late. Get Started Now.!

How to Become a "HOMEOWNERS IN MOTION" Distributor

First, let's examine how HOMEOWNERS IN MOTION works and how you can become a mail order distributor operating from your own home in your spare time.

What Does HOMEOWNERS IN MOTION do for its Clients?

It is a Real Estate Company that offers homeowners, businesses, farms, condominiums and vacation homeowners a proven way to sell their property without the use of a broker.

What is the Selling Price of the HOMEOWNER's Kit, and what is my Profit?

The selling price of the "HOMEOWNERS IN MOTION" Selling Kit is $24. Your profit is $12. You are supplied with advertising for the newspaper or your local yellow pages. You are supplied with 25 mailers (packages) to be mailed to your prospective customers. And you also receive one sample "HOMEOWNERS IN MOTION" KIT.

What Does the "HOMEOWNERS IN MOTION" Kit include...

- 25 forms in all
- "For Sale by Owner" sign

- "Open House" signs
- A book entitled, "How to Sell Your Home Without a Broker" Copyright, Library of Congress, 1977
- Advertising program that works
- How to price your house
- How to get your house ready for sale
- 17 steps in preparing your house to show
- How to advertise in out-of-town newspapers for transfers
- HOUSE INFORMATION SHEETS for your listing
- CHECKLISTS to prepare house for showing
- When and where to get an appraisal
- Market comparison sheet
- Sales Contracts
- Promissory notes
- Binders
- Expense sheet
- Names of mortgage companies
- Confidential buyer information sheets
- Types of loans: FHA, VA, CONV
- Loan amortization tables. Monthly payments
- LIST OF INFORMATION Needed from buyer by mortgage company
- THE TITLE SEARCH and title insurance rates
- How to take back a second mortgage
- 40 ways to professionally negotiate a real estate contract
- Estimated seller's settlement charges
- Purchaser's estimated settlement charges
- Sales Contract Addendum
- SUBJECT TO SALE contingency
- Occupancy agreement
- When and where to get a real estate attorney
- When to get a termite inspection if required
- Information on renting with an option to buy
- Selling techniques on how to market and show your house
- How to complete the sale of your house

How Can I Sell HOMEOWNERS IN MOTION by mail

We supply you with all the required material, which you will need to get started. All you have to do is address the mailers and mail them to a list of prospective clients, which we will show you how to find right in your local newspaper.

Are You Going to Handle All My Clients by Drop Shipping the Kits to Them?

Yes. All kits will be drop-shipped to you or your clients the same day the order is received. You collect $24, keep $12, and send us $12 with your label if you desire. A confirmation notice will be sent to you the same day the kit is mailed.

What Is My Guarantee?

You are covered by a 100% Money Back Guarantee. If, after thirty days of examining our kit, you are not fully satisfied, just mail back the "HOMEOWNERS IN MOTION" Sales Kit and receive a full refund.

How Do I Order the "HOMEOWNERS IN MOTION" Selling Kit?

Simply write on a plain sheet of paper, and address to:

HOMEOWNERS IN MOTION
One Homeowners Plaza
P.O. Box 607, Dept. 1-B
Herndon, VA 22070

I wish to become your Authorized Mail Order Distributor for "HOMEOWNERS IN MOTION". Please send me the following: advertising for newspapers and yellow pages: 25 mailers; and one sample selling kit.

I am enclosing $24.00 check or money order payment in full.
I wish to charge by credit card:

Visa Card # _____ Exp. Date _____

Master Charge # _____ Exp. Date _____

Inter Bank # _____

Name _____ Address _____

City _____ State _____ Zip_____

Signature _____

Company Name _____
(Please print)

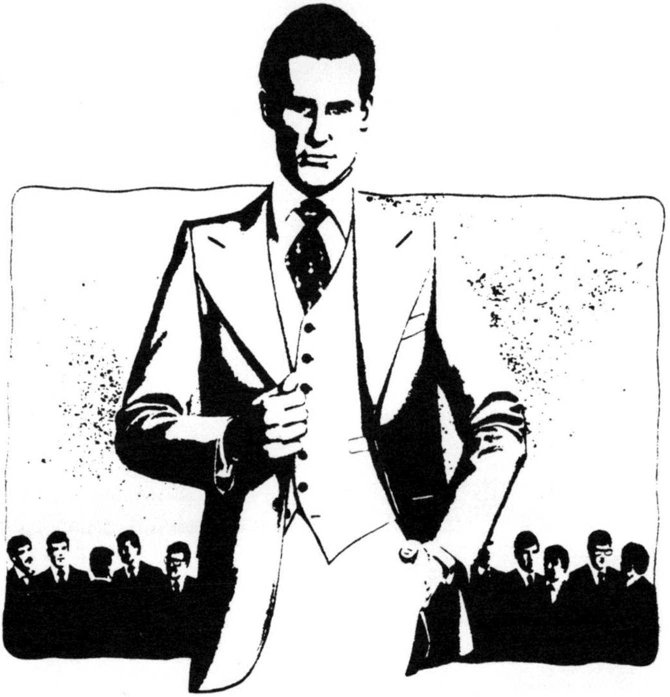

How to Buy a Going Business with No Cash

The little guy takes on a financial giant...and wins.

In some of the books we have read, there are men who succeeded with such violent speed that it might almost be called sinful. Over the years, most people in this country have believed that it takes hard work and years of patience to become a millionaire. Bull! That may have been true 20 years ago, but today it is a whole new ball game. Men who have been slaving away at a nine-to-five job, getting nowhere are starting to wak up and realize that with all the knowledge that this country has, there must be a better way.

Some of the reasons for this fairy tale continuing is that when a man begins to suceed at a faster than normal pace, people start to notice him and generally feel uncomfortable in the presence of instant success. Behind his back people are saying, "How can anyone be that lucky," or simultaneously they are saying, "Why can't it be me? Why does he have to have all the luck?" If you will look deeper into the reson why he is having all the luck, you will find that luck has little to do with it. In most cases you will find a hard working individual with a workable plan in his hand. And you won't find him at home dreaming about how to present this plan or who to present it to. You will find him out in the street presenting his plan to anyone who will listen (bankers, investors, real estate brokers, company presidents, anyone who has the money to back his plan or knows where to acquire the money).

The newest and quickest way to amass a fortune is to buy someone else's troubled company. Fine. How do I do that? Where do I go? Who do I talk to? How much do I offer? And, most of all, Where do I get the money to buy a $44 million company?

To get started, you must look in the major newspapers in this country starting with the: NEW YORK TIMES... WALL STREET JOURNAL... LOS ANGELES TIMES... MIAMI HERALD... SAN FRANCISCO EXAMINER... CHICAGO TRIBUNE... WASHINGTON POST. These are a few of the nation's largest publications. In the classified section, you will find a heading: Manufacturing for Sale or Lease, Business Opportunities, Investment Property for Sale or Lease. Read and cut out all the sections and put them up on your wall in your kitchen or office, or in your home.

Look at them and study them every day. Find one such company operation that interests you, something you feel strongly in. Maybe it's plastic manufacturing, or newspaper publication, or anything to which you feel you can really relate.

Now, find a similar business that is profitable and study what they are doing. Go out and ask to speak to the president. Tell him that you are planning to start a business like his and you would like a few pointers on how he got started (what makes him so successful, etc.). You will find him easy to talk to. (He doesn't know you don't have any money.) He will probably be happy to tell you how he started from scratch and built his business to what it is today. Converse like a news reporter. Have a list of the questions you are going to ask him. Find out about his competition. Maybe he will even tell you how he would run the business that you are planning to purchase. (Do not tell him that you are planning to buy it.)

Once you have talked to enough people (company presidents and the like), you are off to execute your plan. Walk into the company that you are planning to take over and ask to speak to the president (or owner). Tell him that your corporation is interested in buying his business, and that you would like to have a run down on its operating procedures and a list of all of the note holders (lending institutions to which his company owes money). It is a good idea to take along a CPA or accountant who will agree to keep quiet while you are talking. Having a CPA with you lends credibility to your initial fact finding trip.

Now that you have all the information that you need, proceed to the note holders and find out where they stand. Is he behind in his payments? Are they reasonable men with whom to deal? Do they feel that their money is still safe? Try and get a copy of the original contract that he signed in borrowing the money. A good lawyer can find more loop-holes in contracts than one could imagine.

Once all the Information is Collected, Here is the Plan

Start out by laying everything out:
1. Note holders (names, addresses, amount of each note, when it is due).
2. Information that you received from the competition (how he would run the company).
3. Value of the inventory. (Is there too much on hand? Can you sell it?)
4. Value of machinery.
5. Value of the building and land.
6. Accounts receivable.
7. Are there too many employees (payroll).
8. Are the selling or marketing practices outdated.

Once you have analyzed all this information, sit down with an attorney, who is a friend, and your CPA, and start drawing your plan. Keep in mind that it may be more advantageous to present the plan to note holders only than to present it to the owner of the company.

Draw up contracts. Example:
1. Find new ways of satisfying note holders.
2. Offer the president an income for the next 20 years, in lieu of cash at settlement.
3. Take a first or second mortgage on the building.
4. Sell part of the stock you will receive.
5. Sell part of the inventory.
6. Cut down on some of the high payroll executives.
7. Set up a sale/lease back of the equipment.
8. Find a new way to market the product.
9. Split the company into two divisions, and sell stock in the new division.
10. Find a strong collector to get the accounts receivable on time.
11. Offer shares of stock to loyal company employees.

This list could go on and on. If you spend four hours a day for two months or eight hours a day for a year, it is a small price to pay to land a $44 million dollar company.

The following list of companies should be of help to you in making your plan:

SALE/LEASE BACKS

Aetna Life Insurance Co.
151 Farmington Ave.
Hartford, CT 06115

Connecticut Mutual Life Ins.
140 Garden St.
Hartford, CT 06105

Emil Mosbacher
515 Madison Ave.
New York, NY 10022

Home Life Insurance Co.
253 Broadway
New York, NY 10007

Life and Casualty Ins. Co.
Life and Casualty Tower
Nashville, TN 37219

Penn Mutual Life Insurance
530 Walnut St.
Philadelphia, PA 15222

Central Manufacturing District
1 First National Plaza
Chicago, IL 60670

Continental Assurance Co.
310 S. Michigan Ave.
Chicago, IL 60604

Gibson Willoughby, Ltd.
100 University Ave.
Toronto, Ont., Canada

Lambrecht Realty Company
3300 Penebscot Bldg.
Detroit, MI 48226

Nationwide Development Co.
246 N. High St.
Columbus, OH 43215

Prudential Life Insurance Co.
Prudential Mall
Newark, NJ 07102

Ruhl and Ruhl, Inc.
First National Bldg.
Davenport, IA 52801

State Mutual Life Assurance
440 Lincoln St.
Worcester, MA 01605

The Kemper Corp.
60 E. 42nd St.
New York, NY 10017

Travelers Insurance
Securities Department
Hartford, CT 06115

FIRST AND SECOND MORTGAGE COMPANIES

Ballard Mortgage Company
Box 2068
Montgomery, AL 36103
Bankers Mortgage Company
Transamerica Pyramid
San Francisco, CA 94111

Bank of New Mexico
Box 1830
Albuquerque, NM 87103
Benjamin Shore Co.
141 Milk St., Ste. 1143
Boston, MA 02109

C.I. Planning Corp.
717 5th Ave.
New York, NY 10022

Camden Trust Company
Broadway at Market
Camden, NJ 08102

Canada Permanent Trust Co.
1901 Yange St.
Toronto, Ont., Canada

Cauble and Company
811 Fulton Federal Bldg.
Atlanta, GA 30303

Dobson and Johnson, Inc.
Box 17427
Nashville, TN 37217

Dorman and Wilson, Inc.
Box 366 Main Sta.
White Plains, NY 10602

Eastern Mortgage Corp.
1140 Connecticut Ave., N.W.
Washington, DC 20036

Ellison Realty
1720 E. Pacific Cst. Hwy.
Long Beach, CA 90806

Fidelity Investment Company
229 S. Market
Wichita, KS 67202

Finance Corporation
3100 S. Jamestown
Tulsa, OK 74135

First Alabama Financial Corp.
3814 Claridge Rd.
Mobile, AL 36606

First Atlantic Corp.
Box 2665
Charlotte, NC 28234

G. Menitz
Box 217
Madison, WI 53701

Galbreath Mortgage Co.
2940 U.S. Steel Bldg.
Pittsburgh, PA 15219

Gale-Oppenheimer
113 W. Sunrise Hwy.
Freeport, NY 11520

Gem State Realty
Rt. 3, Box 184A
Jerome, ID 83338

Hartzler Mortgage Company
51 E. Gay St.
Columbus, OH 43215

Income Properties, Inc.
5107 Monona Dr.
Madison, WI 53716

Iowa Securities Company
2345 Rice St.
St. Paul, MN 55113

JK Management Associates
1505 Commonwealth Ave.
Brighton, MA 02135

BUSINESS INVESTMENT COMPANIES

Central Invest. Corp. of Denver
811 Central Bank Bldg.
Denver, CO 80202

Allied Capital Corporation
1625 Eye St., N.W.
Washington, DC 20006

Dixie Capital Corporation
2210 Gas Light Tower
Atlanta, GA 30303

Industrial Investment Corp.
413 Idaho St.
Boise, ID 83702

Interscap Capital Corp.
Main St.
Tipton, IN 46072

Commercial Capital, Inc.
Box 939
Covington, LA 70433

Michigan Capital & Service Inc.
410 Wolverine Bldg.
Ann Arbor, MI 48108

Capital Investors Corporation
Capital Building
Missoula, MT 59801
Mor-America Capital Corp.
One First National Center
Omaha, NB 68102

New Mexico Capital Corp.
1420 Carlisle Ave. N.E.
Albuquerque, NM 87110

Hamilton Capital Fund, Inc.
660 Madison Ave.
New York, NY 10021

Continental Capital Corp.
555 California St. Suite 2690
San Francisco, CA 94104

Growth Business Funds, Inc.
2100 E. Hallendale Beach Blvd.
Hallendale, FL 33009

SBIC of Hawaii, Inc.
1575 S. Beretania St.
Honolulu, HI 96814

N. Central Capital Corp.
203 Mulberry St.
Rockford, IL 61105

Mor-America Capital Corp.
200 American Bldg.
Cedar Rapids, IA 52401

Atlas Capital Corp.
55 Court St.
Boston, MA 02108

Vicksburg SBIC
Box 1240
Vicksburg, MS 39180

J & M Investment Corp.
647 West Third St.
Reno, NV 89503
Monmouth Capital Corp.
First State Bank Bldg.
Toms River, NJ 08753

Basic Capital Corp.
40 West 37th St.
New York, NY 10017

Delta Capital, Inc.
320 S. Tryon St.
Charlotte, NC 27609

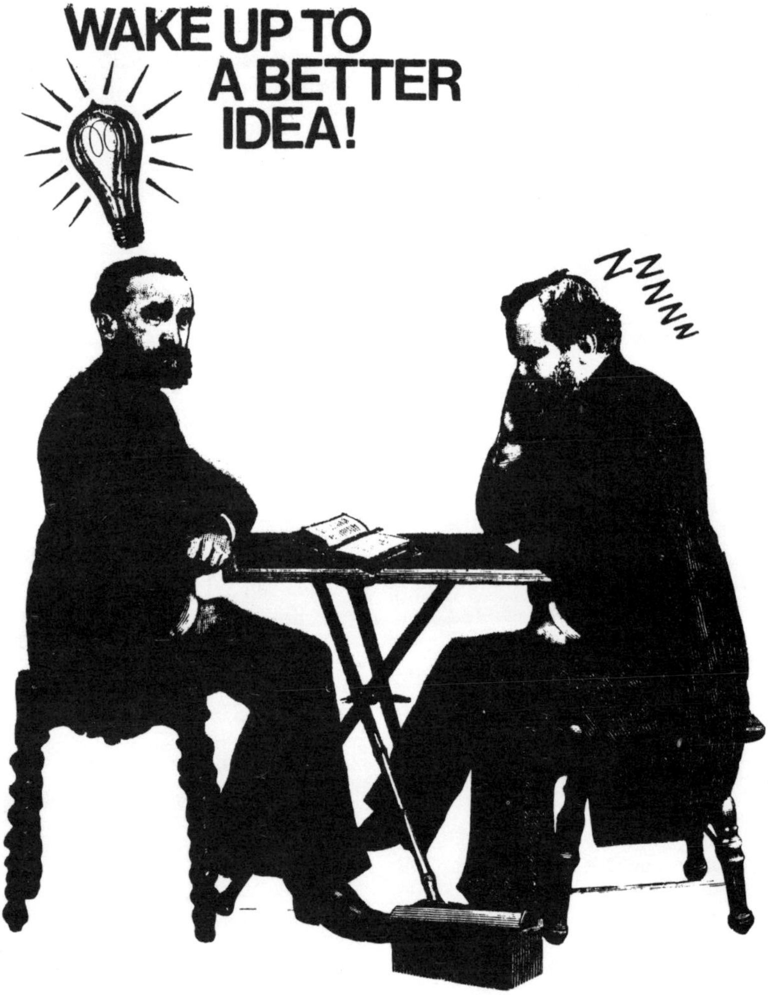
WAKE UP TO
A BETTER
IDEA!
ZZZZZ

How to Buy Land that No One Wants and Lease it to the U.S. Government

Be the King on Top of the World! Buy mountaintops and then lease them to radio stations, television stations, National Weather Service, U.S. Air Force, and state police.

The climb to success will be a short one, if you know what to look for. In this chapter, I will explain how to buy mountaintops for practically no money out of your pocket and lease them for $100 to $700 or more per month.

Let me tell you about a success story in this field. Mr. Loren McQueen in California is making a handsome income buying mountaintops and leasing them to the Government. He started his climb to riches when he paid just over $2,000 for about 270 acres at the top of a mountain outside of San Jose, California. It seemed like everyone including his father wondered if he had gone mad. Today Mr. McQueen owns 73 peaks from Seattle to San Diego with many tenants paying him sky-high rents for sky-high space. Today he claims his acerage is worth over one million dollars.

We recommend that you start out with a good topography map of a major city near your hometown. Mark a large circle of not more than 100 miles from the center of the city. Start searching out mountaintops on the week ends or while on vacation. The harder they are to reach the better. Pick out the highest mountaintops and concentrate on them. Your first objective is to find the owner. This can be done in an informal way by simply knocking on the door of the closest house to the top of the mountain and inquiring if the owner of the house owns the top of the mountain. If they don't, they can probably tell you who does. Don't feel as though you are intruding. First, people generally love to give out information because it makes them feel important. Second, in most cases, you will find the person knows nothing of the possible potential (the secret) of his land.

If you wish to do this in a more formal way, simply take your map with the general area of the mountains you have found marked on it to the nearest court house and request assistance. All properties are recorded in the Office of Records and Deeds. All pertinent information and the owners names are available to the public. Not only will you be able to find the owners name but how much they paid for the property, and when.

With this information as your guide, you should be able to make a good offer when you contact the owner.

Once you have made contact, ask the owner if he would consider selling part or all of his property. You may only need part of the property to make the deal. Also, make sure that you get right of way to the property or you won't be able to use it. Don't become land locked. Be sure to mention how much you are willing to pay for the property and be sure *not* to mention the reason you want it. If the owner says yes right away, then you are ready to make a "preliminary" deal.

You will need a form called an option to purchase, which can be obtained through any office supply store. Fill this form out making the option for 30-60 days, or longer if you can get the owner to agree. Give it to the owner with a promissory note (also can be purchased at an office supply store) for about 1% of the price of the property.

When you start to receive phone calls, drive the interested person to the location. Don't be concerned with the possibility of the prospect meeting the owner because you, and only you, have a legal option to buy the property and no one can side-step you to get the property.

When you have your client signed on a lease (also can be obtained from the office supply), your last step is to return to the owner with a contract (office supply again — standard land contract), and exercise your option to buy the property. You should have no problem borrowing the down payment from a bank provided you show them the lease agreement.

By the way, if the mountaintop that you choose does not suit any of your prospective clients, simply inform the owner that you will not be exercising your option to buy and he is bound by law to cancel your promissory note, so you can never lose any money this way.

You can have an option on as many properties as you like at one time, so feel free to give your clients a wide choice. Happy mountain climbing and money making.

SAMPLE FORM

OPTION TO PURCHASE

_____
Date

It is hereby agreed between _____
Purchaser, and _____
Seller: that the purchaser reserves the option to purchase the
property described below. _____
_____(legal description)_____

This option will be granted to the purchaser for a period of_____
days from the above date. The purchaser will then be required to
exercise this option by a contract to purchase; otherwise, this
option will become null and void without further notice and the purchaser's entire deposit of $_____ (   ),
will be refunded.

Name of Purchaser_____

Address_____

Telephone _____ _____
              (Home)   (Business)

_____
        DATE
_____
        Signature of Purchaser
_____
        Signature of Purchaser

Yesterday!

Tomorrow!

New Mail Order Secret Revealed

For many years it has amazed dealers in the mail-order field that there is so little information or literature on the subject. The business of selling by mail — which includes operations from a Sears Roebuck handling over three billion dollars worth of transactions annually to the little old lady in Pennsylvania who ships 50 dozen cookies at Christmastime each year. Certainly there are hundreds of people in the middle who are making $100,000 or more each year selling by mail.

Down through the years, the recognized experts in the field have developed the art of selling by mail to a high and fine degree. Through the methods of testing each and every advertisement, a definite pattern of result-getting mail-order advertising has appeared that is well worth knowing and remembering.

This chapter contains, in addition to a new mail-order secret, the fundamentals and the results of many of the tests which have been made by mail-order experts. It is based on case histories taken from the files of mail sellers of a wide variety of products, varying size from the smallest to the very largest.

Those who have never sold merchandise or information through mail-order have yet to enjoy the tremendous satisfaction of having consumers respond — immediately — to the magic words. it is this aspect of mail-order work which helps make the advertising business one of the most thrilling in the world. For each mail-order technique is different and it permits the advertiser to see exactly how his prospects react to the stimulus of his appeals. This knowledge is so valuable that it should be part of the standard equipment of every mail-order beginner, and not merely the trade secret of experienced mail-order advertisers.

How Fortunes are Made with the New Mail-OrderSecret

Purchase a copy of the following publications: NATIONAL ENQUIRER... MIDNIGHT... STAR... MECHANIX ILLUSTRATED. You can pick these newspapers and magazines up at your local 7-11 or drug store.

Order the following publications "FREE": Income Opportunities, 380 Lexington Avenue, New York, NY 10017; Salesman's Opportunities, 307 N. Michigan Ave., Chicago, IL 60611; Specialty Salesman, 607 N. Michigan Ave., Chicago, IL 60601; Business Opportunities Journal, 5037 Newport Ave., San Diego, CA 92017.

In writing to these publications, make sure to write c/o the Advertising Department, asking for a FREE copy of their publication and a rate card, for you are planning to advertise in their magazine. They will be more than willing to oblige you.

Now that you have all these publications in your home, find an advertisement in these publications that is going to be your competition. Find one who is selling something that you would like to sell: Ideas, Books, or Products. Let's take an example. Suppose you select ads that are selling "Self-Hypnosis." Search every publication that you have and cut out all the ads that are selling "Self-Hypnosis" and hang them on your wall in your office. Study them to find out how many times they run the ad, how large the ad is, and if it appears in most of the publications. If it does, it is a sure bet that the company advertising the product is doing very well. Now send for each one of the Free Brochures or mail away for the product itself. When you have the products, try and come up with one of your own that is similar to the ones that are successful using your own ideas to make it better than your competition.

Some of the wealthiest mail-order operators are selling printed information by mail. The only initial investment is "Time" in writing the book or booklet and costs of printing the brochures and advertising.

It is interesting to note that some of the largest mail-order book publishers have the smallest portion of its sales in the larger cities, where the greatest number of retail book stores exist to serve its readers. Since metropolitan readers can obtain most books locally at their book shop rather than mail-order. The fact that the great percentage of the mail-order buyers live in a small town and rural areas is explained by the lack of sufficient local book-stores to serve them. In fact, there are hundreds of towns in the country lacking a single bookstore to which literate prospects can go. As one mail-order company expressed it, "We are utilizing 45,000 post offices as book outlets to solve the problem of distribution to non-metropolitan readers."

So you can readily see that if you could get one person to order your book from each post office in the country for $15, and if your profit from each sale is $10, you will net $450,000 a year not counting the orders you may receive from metropolitan dwellers.

Before I go into the specifics of mail-order sellings, let me tell you what one of the successful operators is doing:

A gentleman in California in the early 70's wrote a book entitled, "The Lazy Man's Way to Riches," and marketed his book by means of full page advertising in national magazines and newspapers. Time Magazine wrote an article in 1975 stating that Joe Karbo (author) had made over $500,000 in 1973, and in 1974 by the middle of the year had sold 290,000 copies at $10 each.

Not everyone can start out with full page ads. Some of the successful started with $50 and one classified ad in national magazines and today are making over $100,000 a year by using the pyramiding method.

Pyramiding Method

Making $100,000 a year in the mail-order business is easier than you think. Placing the right ad in the right publication can pyramid your $50 into a fortune. Many successful mail-order practitioners began this way. You can start small and grow as big as you want using the pyramiding method.

Pyramiding works like this: Place an ad in the National Enquirer (classified section) running for one month. At the end of the month take the profits from that ad and purchase two ads (one in the National Enquirer and one in the Globe publication Midnight). As you can see, ad 1 pays for ad 1 and 2, and ad 2 pays for 1, 2, and 3.

Under the right conditions you will be in 20 newspapers and magazines in one year... starting with ony $50 of your own money. The advertising costs comes out of the profits, not out of your pocket.

Perhaps the most popular type of information is How-To-Do something books (Making Money, Starting a New Business or even Having a Better Marriage). These books and self-improvement courses provide valuable information lacking in many towns and even cities across the country. Each book is an individualized product, and to that extent is an exclusive offer.

Make sure that the items or books that you offer are capable of sale to the great mass of people, for they hold the maximum promise of profit. Why this is true is obvious. Any limitation of appeal decreases profit potentials. Although a product or publication need not appeal to every kind of consumer to be profitable, it is evident that the larger the market the greater the profit.

Price Range! Books and products have been sold successfully through mail-order in an extremely wide price range — from $1.45 to $300 or more for a specialized improvement course. There have been instances in which a single unit of machinery costing as much as $3,000 has been sold through the direct mail; there are exceptional cases. One of the very popular price ranges is that which falls between $10 and $35; it is not so steep as to exclude the great market of buyers who may not be able to afford spending a substantial amount, and it is not so low as to permit operating expenses and cost per order to devour most of the gross profit. This is not to say, of course, that merchandise priced outside this range cannot be sold. What is said here is that many mail-order items or books are found within this range. It should be remembered that whether your product or book is priced at $5 or $35, many operating expenses (rent, lights, printing, binding, postage, advertising, wrapping, and handling, etc.) may continue at the same level. Therefore, the mail-order advertiser should select a product or book and a price that will yield a comfortable profit on each sale. For example, if you sell a book at $15, you should realize at least $10 net profit per copy.

Here is accounting of costs applicable to the sale of a book through mail-order, calculated on a per book basis:

Selling Price		$15.00
Cost to have book printed	$ .85	
Advertising expenses, per order	1.90	
Operating expenses	.35	
Postage (brochures)	.15	
Postage, per book	.36	
Box (wrapping)	.28	
Cost to have brochures printed	.95	
Total Cost		4.84
NET PROFIT		$10.16

There is no general rule concerning the extent of markup for any product. Some items are marked up six or seven times over cost of manufacture; others only two to three. It is a good idea never to fall below 3 in selling books. It may be stated, however, that the greater the cost of manufacture the lower the markup should be. If a prospective advertiser proceeds on the assumption that the higher the markup the greater his profit will be, he may be headed for distinct disappointment. As the selling price is increased for any item, there is a corresponding increase in consumer resistance to buy the product.

The Three Methods of Selling by Mail

In the mail-order business there are only three ways to sell your product by mail.

1. Direct from ad... with coupon or order form attached.
2. Inquiry method... mail out brochures.
3. Direct mail... use of mailing lists.

The first method is one most commonly used in mail-order selling. It is the simplest and easiest way to get started. You insert an ad, either display or classified, and use this ad to acquire orders directly from your prospects. Such an ad is usually used for items that do not exceed $10. In some cases it is used effectively at the $15 range, but for an item exceeding $15 in cost it is recommended that you use the Inquiry Method.

The second method, the Inquiry Method, has been found by many advertisers to be more profitable, especially if the product they are selling is in the $25 to $50 range. The ad calls for free information to be sent to the inquirer, containing a complete explanation of the product's benefits, combined with order blank, testimonials, and pictures if possible. This package of literature is more apt to close the deal for a high cost item than a single publication advertisement, which usually lacks sifficient space to incorporate all these selling points.

Point to remember: Never ask for money when you are trying to get inquiries. Asking for 25ᶜ or $1 in an attempt to cover the cost of mailing out the brochures will certainly kill any chances of being successful.

Also, in setting up your advertising budget try to advertise in the same publication with the same ad several times (at least three) for it is not unusual for an ad to pull several times as many names on its third or fourth insertion as it did on the first.

The last method is the Direct-mail method of selling. Direct, meaning exactly what the name implies. It is direct... straight from you to your prospective customer. No advertising costs... no cost to process the inquiries. And, best of all, no waiting 45 days for your ad to come out in the publication. Selling directly is the easiest and least expensive way of doing business, but is very tricky even for the experts in the field.

For example: Suppose you have a book which two million people will logically buy. To go a little further, suppose you composed a sales letter, order form, and testimonials that were good enough to bring $15 per order (gross). And to go one step further, suppose you mailed to 10,000 of these people and received 5% return or $7,500 in orders. (By the way, 5% is not usual for a good mailing list.) This would give you a net profit of $5,000 using the formula that I cited early in this chapter. By the time you had mailed to one-fourth of your prospects, you will have netted yourself $125,000. In short, the only thing between you and a fortune is time because it does take time to mail out two million letters. It's being done all the time but not always with this much profit. Some make a lot less because it depends on circumstances (the right mailing list for your product, the right letter to sell your product, and last the right time of year, winter being the best). Experiment with a small mailing list and your sales letter; I think you will do very well indeed. If you are new in this business, the Direct-from ad or the Inquiry method are a safer bet to start with.

Who to Contact for New Mail Order Products

Just write to these publishers or mail order houses for alist of new products they have to offer: New Products Review, 26 Windmill Road, New York, NY 10504; Unicus Enterprises, P.O. Box 375, Norwalk, CN 968722; World Gift Review, 42 Congress St., Jersey City, NJ 07307; Bullets Atlantic Advetisers, 249 N. Summer St., Adams, MA

For a selection of books to sell, write: Arco Publishing Co., P.O. Box 3383, St. Paul, MN 55101; Publishing Company of America, 407 Lincoln Mall, Miami Beach, FL 33139; Selective Books, Inc., 712 South Missouri Ave., Clearwater, FL 33516; Sentinel Book Publishers Inc., 17-21 E. 22nd St., New York, 10010; World Wide Book Service, 251 Third Avenue, New York, NY 10010; Wilshire Book Company, 8721 Sunset Blvd., Hollywood, CA 90069.

If you wish a list of manufacturers who have mail-order items for sale, write the Consulate of Japan, Korea, and West Germany: Japan, 235 E. 42nd Street, New York, NY 10017; Korea, 720 Fifth Ave., New York, NY 10022; West Germany, 460 Park Ave., New York, NY 10022.

The Leading Mail Order Houses

If you would like to have your product sold by a leading mail-order house without any cost to you, your product will appear in their catalog and you could receive a considerable profit from it. The firms listed here are likely to offer you an opportunity to place your product in their catalog. Just send them a letter and a complete description of your product, and indicate in your letter that it would be an ideal gift to advertise in their mail order catalog. Make sure either to send them a sample product or a camera ready photo so they can reproduce it in their publication. Also state the amount the product is to sell for and the commission they will receive. The following are names of some of the larger mail-order houses in the country:

MAIL ORDER HOUSES

Walter Drake & Sons
Drake Building
22nd St. & Bott
Colorado Spring, CO 80904

A & D Enterprises
101 Monroe St.
Newark, NJ 07105

Fingenhut Product
822 S. Front
Mankato, MN 56001

Lana Lobell
225 W. 34th St.
New York, NY 10001

Mascene Dorte
14 Belle Place
Matawan, NJ 07747

Miles Kimball Company
236 Bond St.
Oshkosh, WI 54901

Foster & Gallahar
6623 N. Galena Rd.
Peoria, IL 61614

Francis-Morris Gifts
P.O. Box 1270
Brooklyn, NY 11201

Galco Sales Co. Inc.
7120 Harvard St.
Cleveland, OH 44105

G & G Research
P.O. Box 8395
Dallas, TX 75205

Glen-Mo Division
44 Trombone St.
Cleveland, MO 64734

Greenland Studios
478 Greenland Bldg.
Miami, FL 33147

Honor House Products Corp.
35 Wilbur St.
Lynbrook, NY 11563

Homespun House
Box 5207
Beverly Hills, CA 90211

J. M. Sales
919 N 6th St.
Phoenix, AZ 85504

SALESMEN'S MAGAZINES
Income Opportunities
229 Park Avenue, S.
New York, NY 10003

Opportunity
875 N. Michigan Avenue
Chicago, IL 60611

Spare Time
5810 W Oklahoma Ave.
Milwaukee, WI 53219

Free Enterprise
1212 Avenue of the Americas
New York, NY 10036

Madison House
419 Greenland Bldg.
Miami, FL 33147

Niresk Industries, Inc.
210 S. Des Plaines St.
Chicago, IL 60606

NU-Products Assn.
Lewis Tower Bldg.
19102

Spencer Gifts, Inc.
Albany Ave.
Atlantic City, NJ 08401

Sunset House Distributing Corp.
3485 S. LaCienega Blvd.
Los Angeles, CA 90016

Taylor Gifts
335 E. Conestoga Rd.
Wayne, PA 19087

Two Brothers, Inc.
808 Washington Ave.
St. Louis, MO 63101

A. W. Wells Mail House
505 W. Coleman Ave.
Hammond, LA 70401

Woodmere Mills, Inc.
336 Putnam
Hamden, CN 06514

Money Making Opportunities
13263 Ventura Blvd.
Studio City, CA 91604

Salesman
307 N. Michigan Ave.
Chicago, IL 60601

Extra Income
363 Seventh Ave.
New York, NY 10001

MECHANICS MAGAZINES

Popular Science
380 Madison Avenue
New York, NY 10017

Popular Mechanics
224 W. 57th Street
New York, NY 10019

Mechanix Illustrated
1515 Broadway
New York, NY 10036

Science and Mechanics
229 Park Avenue, South
New York, NY 10003

SPECIAL INTEREST MAGAZINES

Boating
1 Park Avenue
New York, NY 10016

Fate
500 Hyacinth Place
Highland Park, IL 60035

Field and Stream
383 Madison Avenue
New York, NY 10017

Sports Afield
250 W. 55th Street
New York, NY 10019

Flying
1 Park Avenue
New York, NY 10016

Skiing
1 Park Avenue
New York, NY 10016

Hot Rod
8490 Sunset Blvd.
Los Angeles, CA 90069

Motor Trend
8490 Sunset Blvd.
Los Angeles, CA 90069

Modern Photography
130 E. 59th Street
New York, NY 10022

Outdoor Life
380 Madison Ave.
New York, NY 10017

Popular Electronics
1 Park Avenue
New York, NY 10016

Popular Photography
1 Park Avenue
New York, NY 10016

Modern Bride
1 Park Avenue

Workbasket
4251 Pennsylvania Ave.

New York, NY 10016
Psychology Today
1 Park Avenue
New York, NY 10016

Kansas City, MO 64111
Car and Driver
1 Park Avenue
New York, NY 10016

Cycle
1 Park Avenue
New York, NY 10016

Elementary Electronics
229 Park Avenue S.
New York, NY 10003

Audio
134 N. 13th Street
Philadelphia, PA 19107

Science Digest
224 W. 57th Street
New York, NY 10019

Moneysworth
251 W. 57th Street
New York, NY 10019

Money
Time-Life Bldg/Rockefeller Ctr.
New York, NY 10020

Super-8 Filmaker
145 East 49th Street
New York, NY 10017

ADVENTURE MAGAZINES

Adam Film World
8060 Melrose Avenue
Los Angeles, CA 90046

Man's
355 Lexington Avenue
New York, NY 10017

Man's World
667 Madison Avenue
New York, NY 10021

True Action
667 Madison Avenue
New York, NY 10021

Male
667 Madison Avenue
New York, NY 10021

For Men Only
667 Madison Avenue
New York, NY 10021

Bluebook
235 Park Avenue S.
New York, NY 10003

True
8490 Sunset Blvd.
Los Angeles, CA 90069

Modern Man
8150 N. Central Park Ave.
Skokie, IL 60076

Man's Illustrated
235 Park Avenue S.
New York, NY 10003

Action for Men
667 Madison Avenue
New York, 10021

Stag
667 Madison Avenue
New York, NY 10021

Men
667 Madison Avenue
New York, NY 10021

Saga
13263 Ventura Blvd.
Studio City, CA 91604

Men Today
235 Park Avenue S.
New York, NY 10003

Argosy
420 Lexington Avenue
New York, NY 10017

ENTERTAINMENT MAGAZINES

Playboy
919 N. Michigan Avenue
Chicago, IL 60611

VIP
919 N. Michigan Avenue
Chicago, IL 60611

Gallery
116 E. 27th Street
New York, NY 10016

Players
8060 Melrose Avenue
Los Angeles, CA 90046

Hustler
36 W. Gay Street
Columbus, OH 43215

Club
2 W. 45th Street
New York, NY 10036

Oui
919 N. Michigan Avenue
Chicago, IL 60611

Penthouse
909 Third Avenue
New York, NY 10022

Genesis
120 E. 56th Street
New York, NY 10022

Cavalier
316 Aragon Avenue
Coral Gables, FL 33134

Game
7950 Deering Avenue
Canoga Park, CA 91304

PIX
8060 Melrose Avenue
Los Angeles, CA 90046

NATIONAL NEWSPAPERS

National Enquirer
600 S. East Coast Avenue
Lantana, FL 33462

Midnight
1440 St. Catherine West
Montreal Canada

National Star
730 Third Avenue
New York, NY 10017

National Insider
2711 N Pulaski Road
Chicago, IL 60639

GENERAL INTEREST PUBLICATIONS

National Observer
11501 Columbia Pike
Silver Spring, MD

Esquire
488 Madison Avenue
New York, NY 10022

Holiday
1100 Waterway Blvd.
Indianapolis, IN 46202

New Republic
1244 19th Street, NW
Washington, DC 20036

Parade
733 Third Avenue
New York, NY 10017

Saturday Review
488 Madison Avenue
New York, NY 10022

National Lampoon
635 Madison Avenue
New York, NY 10022

Scientific American
415 Madison Avenue
New York, NY 10017

Gentleman's Quarterly
488 Madison Avenue
New York, NY 10022

Signature
260 Madison Avenue
New York, NY 10016

Wall Street Journal
22 Cortlandt Street
New York, NY 10007

Prevention
33 East Minor Street
Emmaus, PA 18049

National Review
150 E. 35th Street
New York, NY 10016

WOMEN'S MAGAZINES

Vogue
350 Madison Avenue
New York, NY 10017

Woman's Day
1515 Broadway
New York, NY 10036

Harper's Bazaar
717 Fifth Avenue
New York, NY 10022

Ms.
370 Lexington Avenue
New York, NY 10017

McCall's
230 Park Avenue
New York, NY 10017

Seventeen
320 Park Avenue
New York, NY 10022

Mademoiselle
350 Madison Avenue
New York, NY 10017

Glamour
350 Madison Avenue
New York, NY 10017

Redbook
230 Park Avenue
New York, NY 10017

Playgirl
1801 Century Park East
Los Angeles, CA 90067

Family Circle
488 Madison Avenue
New York, NY 10022

True Romance
205 E. 42nd Street
New York, NY 10017

True Experience
205 E. 42nd Street
New York, NY 10017

Expecting
52 Vanderbilt Avenue
New York, NY 10017

Modern Bride
1 Park Avenue
New York, NY 10016

Modern Movies
667 Madison Avenue
New York, NY 10021

My Confession
667 Madison Avenue
New York, NY 10021

Screen Stars
667 Madison Avenue
New York, NY 10021

TV and Movie Screen
355 Park Avenue South
New York, NY 10017

Photo Screen
355 Park Avenue South
New York, NY 10017

Modern Love Confessions
355 Lexington Avenue
New York, NY 10017

TV Star Parade
575 Madison Avenue
New York, NY 10022

Viva
909 Third Avenue
New York, NY 10022

Pageant
Box 704
Rouses Point, NY 12979

True Story
205 E. 42nd Street
New York, NY 10017

True Love
205 E. 42nd Street
New York, NY 10017

Baby Talk
66 E. 34th Street
New York, NY 10016

American Baby
575 Lexington Avenue
New York, NY 10022

American Girl
830 Third Avenue
New York, NY 10022

True Secrets
667 Madison Avenue
New York, NY 10021

Secret Story
667 Madison Avenue
New York, NY 10021

Movie Mirror
355 Park Avenue South
New York, NY 10017

TV Picture Life
355 Park Avenue South
New York, NY 10017

Daytime TV
355 Park Avenue South
New York, NY 10017

TV Radio Talk
575 Madison Avenue
New York, NY 10022

Screen Stories
575 Madison Avenue
New York, NY 10022

Weight Watchers Magazine
635 Madison Avenue
New York, NY 10022

MAIL-ORDER NEWSPAPER SHOPPING SECTIONS

Chicago Tribune Magazine
435 N. Michigan Avenue
Chicago, IL 60611

Los Angeles Times Magazine
Times Mirror Square
Los Angeles, CA 90053

New York Times Magazine
229 W. 43rd Street
New York, NY 10036

Family Weekly
641 Lexington Avenue
New York, NY 10022

Philadelphia Inquirer Today
400 N. Broad Street
Philadelphia, PA 19101

St. Louis Globe Magazine
12th Boulevard and Delmar St.
St. Louis, MO 63101

SHELTER MAGAZINES

House and Garden
350 Madison Avenue
New York, NY 10017

House Beautiful
717 Fifth Avenue
New York, NY 10022

Flower and Garden
4251 Pennsylvania
Kansas City, MO 64111

Better Homes and Gardens
1716 Locust Street
Des Moines, IA 50336

Good Housekeeping
959 Eighth Avenue
New York, NY 10019

American Home
641 Lexington Avenue
New York, NY 10022

MISCELLANEOUS PUBLICATIONS

Army Times (C)
475 School Street, SW
Washington, DC 20024

Air Force Times (C)
475 School Street, SW
Washington, DC 20024

Navy Times (C)
475 School Street, SW
Washington, DC 2024

Ebony
820 S. Michigan Avenue
Chicago, IL 60605

American Legion
1345 Avenue of the Americans
New York, NY 10019

Elks
425 W. Diversey Parkway
Chicago, IL 60614

VFW
406 W. 34th Street
Kansas City, MO 64111

Moose
100 E. Ohio Street
Chicago, IL 60611

Catholic Digest (C)
Box 3090
St. Paul, MN 55165

Writer's Digest (C)
9933 Alliance Road
Cincinnati, OH 45242

Successful Farming (C)
1716 Locust Street
Des Moines, IA 50303

Organic Gardening (C)
33 E. Minor Street
Emmaus, PA 18049

Sepia
1220 Harding Street
Ft. Worth, TX 76102

Jive
1220 Harding Street
Ft. Worth, TX 76102

Hep
1220 Harding Street
Ft. Worth, TX 76102

Bronze Thrills
1220 Harding Street
Ft. Worth, TX 76102

Astrology (C)
600 Third Avenue
New York, NY 10016

Occult (C)
600 Third Avenue
New York, NY 10016

Popular Crosswords (C)
600 Third Avenue
New York, NY 10016

Prairie Farmer (C)
2001 Spring Road
Oak Brook, IL 60521

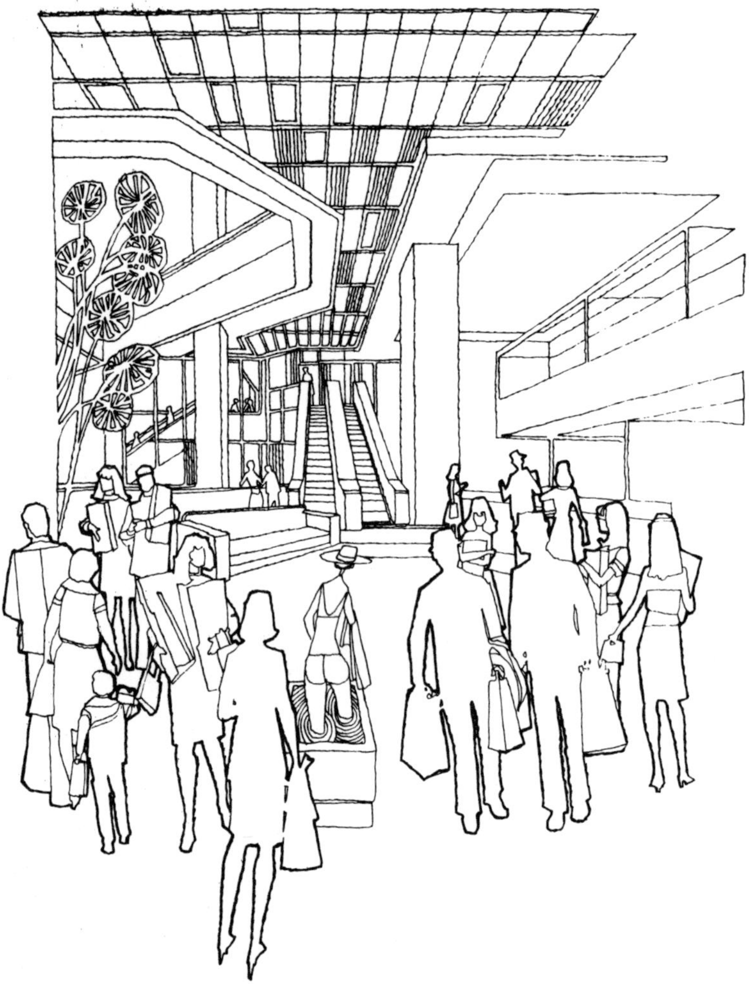

How to Lease a Store in a Shopping Center ... Receive $10,000

Incredible as it may seem there are companies that will give you a check for $5,000, $10,000 and even $15,000 the day you sign a lease in a successful shopping center.

Open an Amusement Arcade

A shopping center mall location is ideal for this business. There are several of these operations opening across the country, but the idea has not spread as fast as you would think. I know that you might say there are amusement centers in every town in the country. But what you probably don't know is that the operators of some of these centers opened with no money out of their own pockets — not one dime.

The reason for this is that there are hundreds of companies that specialize in putting their equipment in a store and will offer you anywhere from 50 to 60 percent of the profits. It costs you nothing and they even provide the maintenance to care for the machines. Most people don't realize that these companies will give you $5,000 to $15,000 (depending on the amount of machines you allow them to put in your store) the day you sign the lease. You are now asking, "Why do they turn over that much money to the owner of the store?" There are several reasons. First, it is reverse selling. What they are doing is paying you your projected commission from the amusement devices in advance. Second, they are keeping out the competition because once you have signed the check you cannot put any other company's machines in your store (not even your own) until the amusement devices have generated enough commission to cover the amount of the check. At that time, the process repeats itself. In fact, you will probably have several companies competing to "give" you money.

The best way to begin in this business is to call several amusement companies which specialize in this type of operation. (I will list some in different parts of the country at the end of this chapter.) Most of them are listed in your yellow pages directory under "Amusement Devices."

You don't have to ask them for the plan when you call. They will offer it to you as soon as you sign the lease.

Retail Business Financed by Amusement Company

If you know a shopping center in which you would like to open a retail business, it will more than pay you to investigate this Golden Opportunity.

For example: If you want to open a restaurant, carry out, sporting equipment shop, or even a book store, and you don't have the cash to start your business, this would be an ideal way of acquiring operating capital.

I personally opened a restaurant (by accident this way) in Washington D.C. (Georgetown). Soon after opening, I found that I was about $5,000 short, and if I didn't raise the $5,000 in 24 hours the restaurant would be closed down and I would be out on the street with my initial investment gone. When! Like a miracle from Heaven, a man appeared at the front door at about 9:00 a.m. in the morning, long before we were ready to open for the day. He stated that he was a salesman from Allied Vending Company, and that he wanted to talk to me about installing some of his vending machines in my restaurant. Well! I can tell you the last person in the world I wanted to talk to at that very moment was a salesman, but I let him in anyway. I needed to talk to someone and quick, or my dreams of being a restaurant owner would be flying right out the window. I came right to the point and told him that I didn't have time to listen to a salesman's pitch because I needed to raise $5,000 in 24 hours, and if he didn't have a solution to offer, to move along. Well, would you believe it, the first words out of his mouth were like a godsend blessing from above. He told me that his company would give me a check for $5,000 tomorrow if I would consent to his company putting in a cigarette vending machine and a juke box in my restaurant. I thought I was hearing things for I couldn't believe that was all there was to it. "Why?" I asked. He told me that his company would pay me an advance on the 50% commission that I would be receiving with the two vending machines installed in my restaurant; and I could have my advance of $5,000 brought to me by 4:00 tomorrow afternoon. The deal was consummated and I received a check for $5,000 along with my vending machines the following day.

Applying this method to your plans of starting a new venture, may be the solution you need. I knew it was for me. Good luck!

VENDING COMPANIES — Washington, D.C., Baltimore

A R Vending and Amusements Inc.
919 Philadelphia
Silver Spring, MD

ARA Food Services
4321 41st
Brentwood, MD

Allied Vending
2120 Beaver Road
Landover, MD

Amusements Unlimited
5601 Annapolis Road
Bladensburg, MD

Atlantic Coin
4002 48th
Bladensburg, MD

Baltimore Cigarette Service
140 St. Azar Avenue
Glen Burnie, MD

Consolidated Vending Co.
6800 Brannon Lane
Chevy Chase, MD

DC Vending Co. Inc.
4115 Kansas Avenue, NW
Washington, D.C.

Executive Vending Co.
2311 Price Avenue
Wheaton, MD

General Vending Sales Corp.
245 W. Biddle
Baltimore, MD

Hunter Vending Co.
1263 1st St., SE
Washington, D.C.

Lou's Vending Service
Wheaton, MD

National Coin Machine Co. Inc.
2410 T Street, NW
Washington, DC

Potomac Vending Services Inc.
9041 K
Gaithersburg, Maryland

B Z Vending
5133-A Frolich Lane
Tuxedo, MD

Bell Coin Machine Co. Inc.
3424 RI Avenue
Mt. Ranier, MD

Custom Vending Co. Inc.
10788 Tucker Street
Beltsville, MD

DC Amusement Co.
10138 Riggs Road
Adelphi, MD

Eyler Vending Inc.
Evergreen Point
Frederick, MD

Hoke Coin Machine Service Inc.
6435 Marlboro Pike
District Heights, Maryland

Jades Vending Corp.
12027 Nebel
Rockville, MD

Montgomery Vending
14612 Woodcrest Drive
Rockville, MD

Postage Service
4263 Howard Avenue
Wheaton, MD

Prince George's Amusements
6435 Marlboro Pike
District Heights, MD

VENDING COMPANIES — Los Angeles

Allied Vending Co.
Phone 873-7200

Amusement Under Glass
12931 Main
Garden Grove, CA

Argo Service Company
P.O. Box 567
Maywood, CA

Automatic Vendors of America
2510 Malt
Los Angeles, CA

Calif Cigarette Concessions
350 W. 130th
Los Angeles, CA

Allied Music Amusement
Phone 873-7200

Anelco Vending Co.
3201 La Cienega
Los Angeles, CA

Automated Vending Co.
Phone 875-1610

Bill & Phill Coin Machines
2277 W. Pico Blvd.
Los Angeles, CA

Coast Vending Corp.
1451 Hooper
Los Angeles, CA

Coffee Caterers
730 E. Florence
Los Angeles, CA

Coffee Club Inc.
5223 Lankershim, NH
Los Angeles, CA

Darvin Corporation
2809 W. Pico
Los Angeles, CA

Family Amusement Corporation
870 N. Vermont
Los Angeles, CA

First Quality Vending
Los Angeles, CA
Phone 674-6463

Harbor Cigarette Service
2020 W. 15th
Long Beach, CA

JB Vending Co.
Los Angeles, CA
Phone 463-4819

M A B Vendors
2121 W. Temple
Los Angeles, CA

National Juice Vendors
7612 Katella
Stanton, CA

Northwest Fruit Co.
7800 Burnet
Van Nuys, CA

Rowe Vending Machines
1433 W. Pico
Los Angeles, CA

Seeburg Vending Machines
2225 W. Pico
Los Angeles, CA

VENDING COMPANIES — New York City

A to Z Vending Services Corp.
30 W. 15
New York, NY

A & V Vending
210 W. 155
New York, NY

Academy Vending Corp.
662 E. 236th St.
Bronx, New York

ARA Services
6 Corporate Park Drive
White Plains, New York

ASCOA
239-19 Braddock Ave.
Bellrose, NY

BAVCO Inc.
73 Warren St.
New York, NY

Bureau Vending Inc.
19-25 Ditmars Blvd.
Astoria, NY

Canteen Food & Vending
3505 Conner
Bronx, NY

Fawn Vending Sales of NY
44 Lincoln Avenue
New Rochelle, NY

Futterman T & H Vending Corp.
1759 Mad Avenue
New York, NY

G & K Vending Co.
12-14 31 Ave.
L.I. City, NY

G & W Vending Inc.
319 W. 48 Street
New York, NY

Guadraphonic Mini Theatres
200 W. 49
New York, NY

Icy-Soda Inc.
1343 Ogden Avenue
Bronx, NY

Jardso Vending Corp.
58-71 54 St.
Maspeth, NY

Lessing's Inc.
75 Spring
New York, NY

Operators Vending Machine
 & Supply
901 Grand St.
Brooklyn, NY

Playland Music & Cigarette
94-29 44 Avenue
Elm, NY

Roy's Vending Co.
3000 Bronx Park
East Bronx, NY

Paramount Automatic Industries
421 Bruckner Blvd.
Bronx, NY

Rowe Corp.
31 E. 17
New York, NY

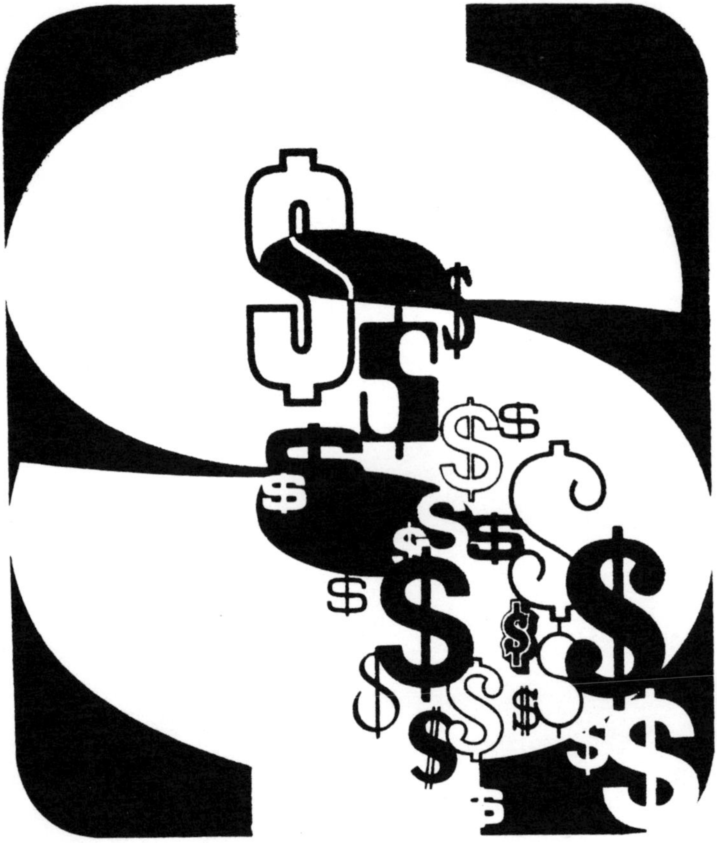

How to Form Your Own Corporation ... for Less Than $60

Sole Proprietor .... Individual ownership.
Partnership .... Two or more owners
                                       acting as partners
Corporation .... A separate and distinct entity.
                                 No owners. Only stockholders.

These are the only three ways for a person or persons to conduct any form of business in this country. Two of them are risky in respect to the personal liability that is in jeoparty. Operating as a sole proprietorship or a partnership can cost you everything you have worked for all your life, if you make one mistake. If your business were to become unprofitable and there was no way for the business to recover and to pay its creditors, you and your partners would become fully liable for all debts incurred within the operation of the business. This means that you could lose your home, car, any money you may have in your savings account, even personal property that you may own in another state clear across the country.

Forming a corporation is by far the safest way to operate any form of business. Small or large, working out of your home or out of a $100,000 office, conducting your business under a corporation name is the safest way to protect your personal liability. What this means is that a corporation is recognized in every state as a separate and distinct entity, leaving only the corporation liable for the debts it may incur. You still may operate your business or company in any way you see fit by being the controlling stock holder.

Here are Some of the Benefits of Owning a Corporation

1. Your personal liability is limited to only the original money you put into the corportion to form it (with exception to state and federal taxes)
2. By forming a corporation, you will be able to enjoy several tax brackets that only apply to stockholders of a corporation. For example: Under "Sub-chapter S" you are not required to pay social security taxes.
3. When trying to raise venture capital, having a corporation is more advantageous to the lenders. By offering them stock in your corporation, you give them a feeling of security and limited

control of how their money is to be used. When paying back your lenders, owning a corportion gives you much more latitude. You can offer repayment in the form of common stock, preferred stock, or dividends. Owning a sole-proprietorship or partnership offers only one solution, CASH!
4. If the corporation fails, you can deduct up to $25,000 on your personal tax return.
5. For the entire set of information books regarding corporations and the tax advantages, write to the IRS, Washington, DC. Make sure to request the book about "Sub-chapter S" corporations and how to qualify to become one.

Where and How to Incorporate

One would assume that his own home state would be the logical choice of where to incorporate, but there are some difficulties in forming a corporation in some of the states. Some states require $1000 as minimum capitalization to form a corporation. Other states require that you have at least two people (sometimes three) to form a corporation, and that no one person can hold two titles in the corporation. This means that you would have to have someone to be the president (yourself) and someone else to be the secretary (maybe your wife) and still a third party to be treasurer (a friend).

Where

I recommend Delaware as the state in which to incorporate. There are many reasons such as the following:
1. To incorporate in the state of Delaware, you don't need three people. You alone can hold the titles of president, secretary and treasurer in your corporation.
2. There are no minimum capitalization requirements. You can form a corporation with no capital, if you desire.
3. Delaware is the only state in which you can form a corporation and not give your name as the incorporator. You can operate the corporation anonymously.
4. All details, while forming the corporation, can be handled by mail. You never have to visit the state.
5. Stockholders are not subject to taxation by the state. Your corporation is exempt from state corporation tax if you are a non-resident.
6. You may assign any value to the stock in your corporation.
7. Delaware does not require you to spell out in detail the exact proposed business activities which the corporation plans to use.
8. The state of Delaware allows you to operate as a non-resident. Most states won't.

How

Incorporating in the state of Delaware is relatively simple requiring only a few procedures:

1. Arrange for a street address that will provide you with a place for public inspection of a certified copy of your Certification of Incorporation. This can be handled by acquiring the services of one of the many Registered Agents in the state of Delaware. I will list several at the close of this chapter.
2. You must file two copies of your Certification of Incorporation with the Secretary of State in the state's capitol. This will all be handled by your Registered Agent (copy shown).
3. You must have a corporate seal, a corporate minutes book, and stock certificates made out with your corporation name on them. All of these forms can be purchased from a local offical store or your accountant will know where to send for them. Normal cost is $25.

Once you have found a registered agent, send him two copies of your Certificate of Incorporation. A sample of one appears in this chapter. The filing fees will be as follows: Filing...$25. Franchise Fee...$10. Certified copy for Registered Agent...$7. Recording of the Corporation...$4. Total...$46.

Registered Agents

Corporation Registry Co.
900 Market Street
Wilmington, Delaware

National Corporation Co.
Keith Building
Dover, Delaware

States Charters Corp.
The Green
Dover, Delaware

Delaware Charter Co.
1314 King Street
Wilmington, Delaware

Incorporators of Delaware
48 The Green
Dover, Delaware

Corporation Service Co.
1314 King Street
Wilmington, Delaware

Registrar and Transfer Co.
306 South State Street
Dover, Delaware

Corporate Planning, Inc.
Box 1187
Wilmington, Delaware

United Corporate Services
26 The Green
Dove, Delaware

CERTIFICATE OF INCORPORATION

of

_____

The name of this corporation is _____

Its registered office in the State of Delaware is to be located at _____
_____ in the _____ County of _____
_____. The registered agent in charge thereof is _____
_____
_____ at _____
The nature of the business and, the objects and purposes proposed to be transacted, promoted and carried on, are to do any or all the things herein mentioned, as fully and to the same extent as natural persons might or could do, and in any part of the world, viz:
"The purpose of the corporation is to engage in any lawful act or activity for which corporations may be organized under the general Corporation Law of Delaware."
FOURTH. — The amount of the total authorized capital stock of this corporation is _____

The name and mailing address of the incorporator is as follows:

NAME: ADDRESS:

The Directors shall have power to make and to alter or amend the By-Laws; to fix the amount to be reserved as working capital, and to authorize and cause to be executed, mortgages and liens without limit as to the amount, upon the property and franchise of the Corporation.

With the consent in writing, and pursuant to a vote of the holders of a majority of the capital stock issued and outstanding, the Directors shall have the authority to dispose, in any manner, of the whole property of this corporation.

The By-Laws shall determine whether and to what extent the accounts and books of this corporation, or any of them shall be open to the inspection of the stockholders; and no stockholder shall have any right of inspecting any account, or book or document of this Corporation, except as conferred by the law or the By-Laws, or by resolution of the stockholders.

The stockholders and directors shall have power to hold their meetings and keep the books, documents and papers of the corporation outside of the State of Delaware, at such places as may be from time to time designated by the By-Laws or by resolution of the stockholders or directors, except as otherwise required by the laws of Delaware.

It is the intention that the objects, purposes and powers specified in the third paragraph hereof shall, except where otherwise specified in said paragraph, be nowise limited or restricted by reference to or interference from the terms of any other clause or paragraph in this certificate of incorporation, but that the objects, purposes and powers specified in the third paragraph and in each of the clauses or paragraphs of this charter shall be regarded as independent objects, purposes and powers.

I, THE UNDERSIGNED, for the purpose of forming a Corporation under the laws of the State of Delaware, do make, file and record this Certificate, and do certify that the facts herein are true; and I have accordingly hereunto set my hand.
DATED AT: _____   _____
State of _____
County of _____

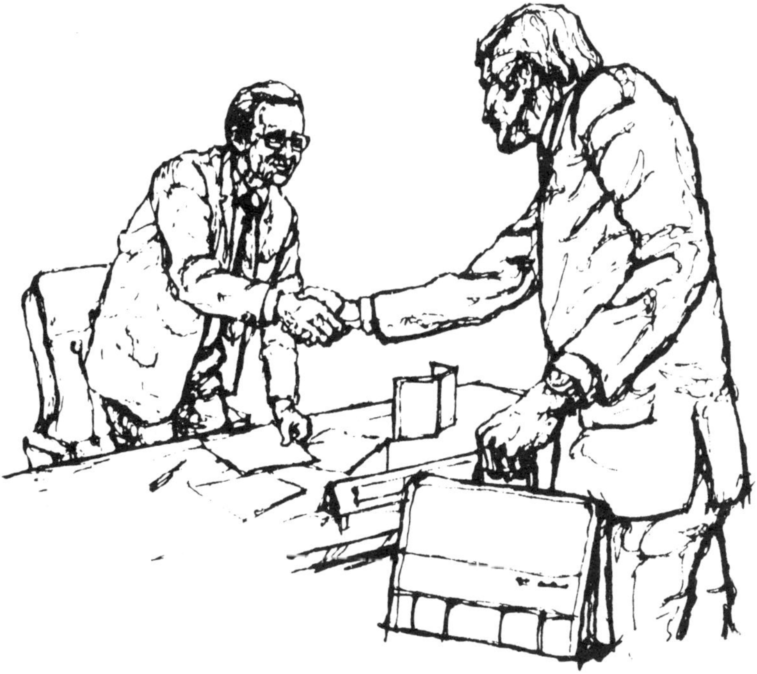

How to Become a Book Critic

Smart money people start with a shelf of good books. When you first begin your search for quick riches, you will probably have few friends or neighbors who will understand you and your new goals. If you are married, your wife or husband may not be too interested in the methods which you will use, but it is certain they wil be interested in the results. This is a common situation — don't worry about it. You need knowledge and business partners. You can easily acquire what some men and women believe are the best friends and business partners in the world: good business books!

If you choose opening your own business or going after a high-paying job, whichever is the best promise of quick wealth, you need books on your particular business or profession. No mater what business it may be, from selling shoes to building a whole city, there is a good book, article, catalog, pamphlet, or other printed document discussing it. All you need is to locate it. What better way than to have the major publishers sending you a copy of their latest publication?

You should divide your library into two parts: first, pleasure reading, such as novels, science fiction, philosophy, westerns, religion, etc.; second, business references. Your business library should be further subdivided into (1) general information on job procedures, billing, records, taxes, etc., or company organization, personnel practices, financial analysis, etc., depending on the method you choose to build your fortune, and (2) specific information on the business or job you choose. This section of your library will reflect your individual interests and will provide valuable dollar-generating ideas you can use for years. In my own quick fortune-building efforts, all of which have been outstandingly successful, several specialized books selling at prices of $5 ro $40 each have returned more than $10,000 income each. This is a return of over 2,000 percent! How can one question the financial value of a good business library? Remember, when first starting a search for your fortune, good business books may be your only friend.

Study each of the books carefully, and you may be able to duplicate Mrs. M's feat. Starting from scratch, never having owned a business before, she built a million-dollar greeting-card business in three years. Her first office was in the basement of her home. As the business grew, she had to move to a warehouse.

Exposition Press Inc.
900 S. Oyster Bay Rd.
Hawksville, NY

Fawcett Publications Inc.
1515 Broadway
New York, NY

Forbes Inc.
60 Fifth Avenue
New York, NY

Time-Life Libraries Inc.
1271 Avenue of the Americas
New York, NY

Unipub
630 First Avenue
New York, NY

Universal Publishing &
Distributing Co.
235 E. 45th
New York, NY

Vintage Books
201 E. 50th
New York, NY

Wonder Books
51 Madison Avenue
New York, NY

Harper & Row Publishers Inc.
10 E. 53rd
New York, NY

David McKay Co. Inc.
750 Third Avenue
New York, NY

Monarch Press Div. of
Simon & Shuster Inc.
1 W. 39th
New York, NY

North Holland Publishing Co.
52 Vanderbilt Avenue
New York, NY

Pageant-Poseidon Press Ltd.
155 E. 15th
New York, NY

Farnsworth Publishing Co. Inc.
78 Randall Avenue
Rockville Center
New York, NY

Studio Publications
625 Madison Avenue
New York, NY

Trident Press Division of
Simon & Schuster Inc.
630 Fifth Avenue
New York, NY

Vanguard Press Inc.
424 Madison Avenue
New York, NY

Viking Press Inc.
625 Madison Avenue
New York, NY

Western Publishing Co.
850 Third Avenue
New York, NY

Youth Education Systems Inc.
49 Gleason Avenue
Stamford, CN

Masson Publishing USA Inc.
14 E. 60th
New York, NY

Monarch Books Inc.
529 Fifth Avenue
New York, NY

New Dimensions Publishing Co.
151 W. 25th
New York, NY

Oxford Book Div. of
W. H. Sadlier Inc.
11 Park Place
New York, NY

Pantheon Books
201 E. 50th
New York, NY

Pathfinder Press Inc.
410 West
New York, NY

Pinnacle Books Inc.
275 Madison Avenue
New York, NY

Pocket Books
Ace Distribution Corp.
1. W. 39th
New York, NY

Random House Inc.
201 E. 50th
New York, NY

Russell & Russell Publishers
122 E. 42nd
New York, NY

Wm. H. Sadlier Inc.
11 Park Place
New York, NY

Sky Books Press Ltd.
48 E. 50th
New York, NY

Pergamon Press Inc.
Fairview Park
Elmsford, New York

Playmore Inc.
1107 Broadway
New York, NY

Prentice-Hall Inc.
U.S. Highway No. 9
Englewood Cliffs, NJ

Rowman & Littlefield Div. of
Littlefield Adams & Co.
81 Adams Drive
Totowa, NJ

Rutledge Books
25 W. 43rd
New York, NY

Simon & Schuster Inc.
630 Fifth Avenue
New York, NO

Springer Publishing Co.
200 Park Avenue
New York, NY

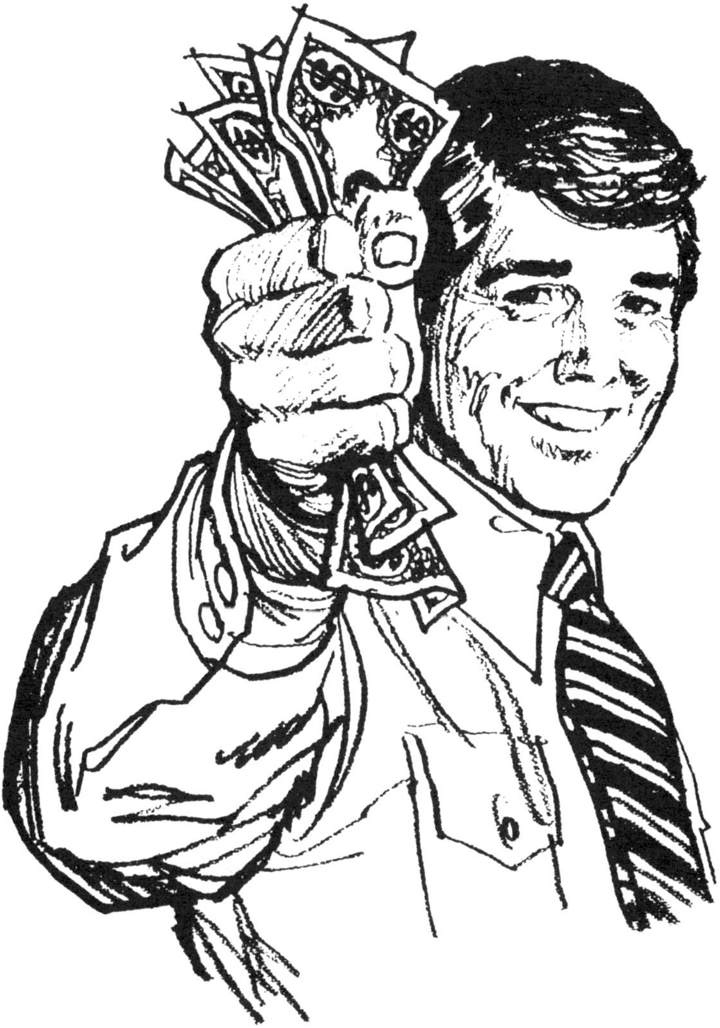

How to Become a Financial Broker... Earning $100,000 a Year

It's probably hard for you to believe at this very moment, but it's A True...Fact! Within 30 days from now, you could be well on your way to earning $100,000 or more as a Financial Broker. There are a few details that you must do first. The advantage is that you can start your new venture from your own home and never have to leave your present employment.

This business is fast becoming one of the most lucrative ways to become wealthy, virtually overnight. Financial brokers in this country are earning more money than anyone else in their field (e.g. contractors, builders, and even some developers). The reason for this sudden rise in income is due to the fact that almost every form of construction going on in this country requires capital. And being a Financial or Mortgage Broker virtually makes you a valued commodity, sought after by every developer and investor in this country.

Before we go on, let me explain that once you are established in this business, you are not limited to only the state in which you reside. You can operate nationwide, and can place loans in any one of the 52 states in this country.

What is Needed to Start?

Item	Amount	Cost
Business Cards	500	$10.00
Quality Stationery (letterheads)	500	20.00
Envelopes #10	1000	25.00
Legal Files	200	20.00
Manila Envelopes (15" x 12")	100	10.00
Company Telephone		26.00 per month

Advertising

Run an ad simlar to this one in your local newspaper for at least three days per week (money permitting) weekdays only. The ad should appear in the business section and should run for at least one month.

> UNLIMITED FUNDS AVAILABLE
> ON
> INCOME PRODUCING PROPERTIES
> $250,000 to $50 million
> available for:
> Business — Developers
> Shopping Centers — Apartments
> Motels — Plants
> Office Buildings — Hospitals
> Trailer Parks — Gas Stations
> Retail Stores
> ABC MORTGAGE COMPANY
> Phone 224-7654
> Sam Miller

This ad will bring you in contact with builders, contractors, developers, and prominent investors, who are all looking for additional capital to finance one of their new ventures. After having advertised in the newspaper for 30 days, you will have more leads than you can handle. Your job will be to weed out the BS'ers and dreamers and to find people who qualify for the amount they are requesting.

Relax! A little practice and this will be like second nature to you. You will be able to spot the phonies with a few choice questions over the phone in your initial interview.

How to Make Money as a Financial or Mortgage Broker

The individuals who will be responding to your advertisement in the newspaper are always in need of additional money for expansion and new development.

This is a partial list of properties that you can handle as a mortgage broker:

— Apartments — Churches — Farm Loans — Bowling Alleys — Construction — Factories — Machinery — Inventory — Second Mortgage Home Loans — First Mortgage Home Loans — Motels — Hotels — Shopping Centers — Debt Consolidation — Office Buildings.

You will find as a mortgage broker you will be able to handle their every need, from $5,000 to $500 million. Your fee will be anywhere from 1% to 4% of the amount loaned.

Here is an example of what you can expect to make:

A broker placed a loan for a 400-unit apartment house. Amount borrowed was $2,400,000. His fee was 1%—$24,000. Time spent by broker putting his package together was three months.

Another broker placed a loan for a small shopping center. Amount borrowed $750,000. His fee was 4%...$30,000. Time spent putting this deal together was 4½ months.

These fees are not unrealistic. Some brokers only work six months out of the year, and vacation in the Caribbean the rest of the year. Keep in mind the fees are always paid the moment your client signs the mortgage.

How to Get Started

Location

The actual location of your office is not important since most of your business transactions will either be handled over the phone or at your prospective client's office (so you will be able to get a more accurate picture of your client's current operation). It is suggested, though, that you set up a separate phone and business answering service, which can be found in the yellow pages under "Telephone Answering."

License

In most states there is no requirement for a license as a Financial Broker. However, there is a license requirement by most states to operate any form of business. The safest way is to call your county court house for local regulations.

Office Supplies

I have already listed the supplies that you will need to start, but it is a good idea to have access to a good copier and to own a new advanced calculator. If you call at a business machines store, I am sure they will be able to recommend those machines that will fit your needs.

Credit Reports

In your new business as Mortgage Broker, you will be required to submit a credit report on each applicant. This will help the lending institution evaluate your client. The initial report costs $16 which you charge your client in advance...non-refundable. This is a normal procedure that all mortgage brokers use. In fact, most charge $100...non-refundable for service fees and the credit reports.

Yellow Page Advertising

It is always a good idea to get into the yellow pages as soon as possible. If your idea is a tri-state area, make sure you are in all three books. For this soon will be your most valuable source of income. The following is a sample ad:

LOANS $5,000 to $500,000,000
Second Mortgage...Business...Commercial
ABC MORTGAGE COMPANY
1845 Main Street...441-3489

Out of Town Directories

Order a yellow page directory from every major city in this country. They are free of charge, and will be invaluable to you in processing the loan packages. Here is a list of major cities:

Los Angeles
San Francisco
New York City (Manhattan)
Miami
New Orleans
St. Louis
Washington, D.C.
Denver

Salt Lake City
Richmond
Houston
Memphis
Dallas
Philadelphia
Tulsa
Cleveland
Atlanta

These directories will give you access to most of the major mortgage sources in the country.

What is the First Step...
Once I am Ready to Go

Your first step is to collect this information in the initial phone call.

1. Amount requested _____
2. How is the money to be used _____
3. How many years do you want to borrow the capital _____
4. How high can you go on monthly payments _____
5. What collateral do you have to pledge for the loan _____
6. Name _____
   Address _____
   Phone _____
7. Company Name _____
   Company Address _____
   Phone _____
8. Social Security Number _____
9. Company Federal ID number _____
10. Name of bank (personal) _____
    Branch _____
11. Name of bank (company) _____
    Branch _____

Once you have all this information, make two phone calls: one to his bank and one to his company's bank. Identify yourself and ask for the branch manager. Tell him that your company is considering financing a new venture for Mr. Jones, and you were wondering if he had a verbal recommendation for or against Mr. Jones and his company. If the branch manager has anything negative to say about Mr. Jones and his company he will tell you, believe me. If everything looks good so far, call the credit bureaus and ask for a verbal on any past due accounts Mr. Jones may have. They will either tell you he has a good rating or 30 days past due, 90 days past due, etc. etc. If he is not bankrupt and he has not skipped any accounts, then you have a valuable client. Late pay notices can be worked out.

The Loan Package

Make an appointment with your client to meet him at his office so you can see his company and have access to papers and information that he will be needing to present the loan to the principle lending company.

This is the information that you will need to present the loan:
1. Pictures of company, if the loan is to be used for expansion.
2. Pictures or plans (drawings) of proposed construction.
3. Credit Report.
4. Personal Financial Statement on all officers of the corporation.
5. Corporation profit and loss statements.
6. Placement Agreement.
7. Summary Sheet.

How to Place the Loan

You begin by calling several mortgage lenders in your area announcing to them that you are a mortgage company and are inquiring in reference to the type of loans that they handle or might be interested in. They will indicate to you the ones they are not interested in. Once you have a good idea what they are looking for, then you submit a package to them, being sure that your initial interview is done in person. If they are interested, they will probably have a few other items you must provide before the loan is approved. Example: Appraisal... Profit and Loss Statements for the last five years... Accounts Receivable... History Background... etc.

Once the package is accepted by the lender, they will give your client every consideration. If the loan is approved, you will be notified. If it is rejected, the package will be returned to you. It is your job to shop it with as many lenders as you feel necessary in order to get it approved, not only in your home state but out of state also. (Out of state lenders don't require a face to face meeting the first time you submit an application.) Usually, after about five rejections you can feel sure that the loan will not be accepted. If this turns out to be the case, you will have not lost anything but time for the $100 that your client gave you is non-refundable.

Tips to Remember

All replies from lenders should be back in one to two weeks. Never submit an application without the $100 fee paid to you in advance. Never submit a loan package to more than one lender at a time. Make sure to always have your placement Agreement signed and your signature notarized. (One signature notarized is all that is needed to make it legally binding on both parties.)

Brokers Fee Schedule

7% fee loans 5,000 to 15,000
5½% fee loans 16,000 to 25,000
5% fee loans 26,000 to 50,000
4% fee loans 51,000 to 100,000
3½% fee loans 101,000 to 200,000
2% fee loans 301,000 to 499,000
2% fee loans 201,000 to 300,000
1½% fee loans 301,000 to 49,000
1% fee loans 500,000 to 10,000,00 and over

R E P L Y   C A R D

Lender_____

Address_____

City and State_____ Zip____

Loan Officer_____

Phone_____

Will invest in the following type of loans:

( ) Motels   ( ) Apartment Houses
( ) Hotels   ( ) Office Buildings
( ) Rest Homes   ( ) Houses
( ) Hospitals   ( ) General Finance
( ) Service Stations ( ) Sub-divisions
( ) Warehouses   ( ) Factoring
( ) Bowling Alleys   ( ) Others_____
( ) Shopping Centers ( ) _____
( ) Machinery   ( ) _____
( ) Farms   ( ) _____

Loan Amounts $_____
Interest_____%
Terms_____yrs

Commission paid by:
    ( ) Lender   ( ) Borrower

2nd mortgages available ( ) yes   ( ) no

_____

Remarks from Investor:_____
_____
_____
_____
_____

PERSONAL FINANCIAL STATEMENT

HUSBAND Birthdate ____ Dependents _____
(Ages) _____

Name: _____
Address: _____
Phone: _____
Social Security No: _____
Employed By: _____
Address: _____

Occupation: _____
Salary: (Gross) $ _____ No of years: _____
Overtime: _____ Phone: _____

PREVIOUS EMPLOYMENT, if on present job less than two years:
Employed by: _____
Address: _____

Occupation: _____
Salary: (Gross) $ _____ No of years: _____
Reason for leaving: _____

WIFE Birthdate ____ Housewife _____
Name: _____
Address: _____

Social Security No: _____
Employed By: _____
Address: _____

Occupation: _____
Salary: (Gross) $ _____ No. of years: _____
Phone: _____

EXTRA EMPLOYMENT OF HUSBAND AND/OR WIFE, if applicable:
Employed by: _____
Address: _____

Occupation: _____
Salary: (Gross) $ _____ No. of years: _____
Phone: _____
Other extra income: (If applicable)
Reserve unit: $ _____ Disability: $ _____
Investments: $ _____ Remarks: _____
Rental Income: _____
Other: _____

****

ASSETS:	Type of Account		LIABILITIES	TOTAL	Monthly Payment
Bank accounts (Name)	(Savings/Check)	Bal. on dep.	Automobile:	$ _____	$ _____
		$ _____		$ _____	$ _____
		$ _____	Property	$ _____	$ _____
		$ _____		$ _____	$ _____
		$ _____		$ _____	$ _____

U.S. Savings Bonds: $ _____
Stocks or other Bonds: (Current Value) $ _____
Life Insurance: (face value) $ _____
Cash surrender value of Ins. $ _____
Property Owned: Current Value

Payments made to _____

Address: _____
Equity: $ _____ $ _____

Other (installment accounts, etc.)
 Balance Due   Monthly Payment

Address: _____
Equity: $ _____ $ _____

Address: _____
Equity: $ _____ $ _____

Household furnishings: (current value) $ _____
Automobile: Yr ____ Make ____ $ _____
Automobile: Yr ____ Make ____ $ _____
Other assets: _____ $ _____
Unusual remarks: _____

Support payments (Alimony, parents)
$ _____

Rent payments: $ _____

****

What is source of money needed for down payment and settlement charges (bank accounts, bonds, insurance, etc. _____

The foregoing information is true and accurate to the best of my knowledge and belief.

SIGNED: _____ (SEAL)   SIGNED: _____ (SEAL)

Sample Forms to be Used
In presenting your Proposal to the Banks

1. APPLICANT _____ PHONE _____
2. ADDRESS _____
3. AUTHORIZED OFFICER _____
4. ADDRESS _____ PHONE _____
5. PURPOSE OF LOAN _____
6. AMOUNT REQUESTED _____ TERM _____
7. SECURITY TO BE PLEDGED _____ 1ST ( ) 2ND ( ) OTHER ( )
8. LOCATIONS OF SECURITY _____
9. APPRAISED OR FACE VALUE OF SECURITY _____
10. ASSETS _____
11. LIABILITIES _____
12. NET PROFIT OR NET LOSS LAST 5 YEARS (show loss figures in parentheses) _____ _____ _____ _____ _____
13. NET WORTH LAST 5 YEARS

_____ _____ _____ _____ _____

LOAN PACKAGE SHOULD HAVE DOCUMENTS LISTED BELOW.
INCLUDE AS MANY AS POSSIBLE ON PROJECT.

14. ( ) LEASE COPIES
15. ( ) MAPS
16. ( ) PICTURES
17. ( ) M.A.I. APPRAISAL
18. ( ) BALANCE SHEET
19. ( ) PROFIT & LOSS STATEMENTS
20. ( ) HISTORICAL BACKGROUND
21. ( ) PLAT
22. ( ) SPECIFICATIONS

23. ( ) DEEDS
24. ( ) CREDIT REPORTS
25. ( ) FINANCIAL STATEMENTS
26. ( ) IMPROVEMENT BIDS
27. ( ) EXISTING MORTGAGE VERIFICATIONS
28. ( ) ITEMIZED COST & VALUE LIST
29. ( ) OTHER _____
30. ( ) OTHER _____

REMARKS _____
_____
_____
_____

SUMMARY COVER SHEET

PLEASE NOTE: It is very important that each question is answered in full.

FROM: _____

BROKER: _____

_____ PHONE/CODE: _____

PROJECT:
    Name:
    Specific Address:
    City & State:

TYPE OF PROJECT:

CURRENT STATUS OF PROJECT: (existing, # years old, proposed construction)

LOAN APPLICANT:
    Name:
    Specific Address:
    City & State:
    Net Worth:
    (Include financial statements and indicate if principals will sign personally)

LOAN REQUESTED:
    Purpose:
    Type: (first, second, standby or other)
    Amount:
    Maturity Terms:
    Interest Rate:

EXISTING FINANCING:
    Name of Lender:
    Address:
    Amount: Rate: Terms:
    Due Date:

(continued)

VALUE OF SECURITY OFFERED: (Continuation of Summary Cover Sheet)
Land: Cost $_____or appraisal_____
Square Feet_____Date bought, optioned or escrowed _____
Improvements: Cost $_____or appraisal_____
Total Value: Cost $_____or appraisal_____

DETAILS: (Important to answer all applicable questions)
LAND DEVELOPMENT. Water_____sewer_____
Roads_____utilities_____
Other_____
Building: Type of Construction_____
# of Buildings_____# of Stories_____Total Sq. Ft._____
# of Units_____Rent Per Unit_____Debt Per Unit_____
# of Rooms_____Rent Per Room_____Debt Per Room_____
Studios_____@ $_____Sq. Ft._____
1 BR_____@ $_____Sq. Ft._____
2 BR_____@ $_____Sq. Ft._____
Other_____
Air Cond_____Elevators_____Parking_____Pool_____
Other_____

ABILITY OF PROJECT TO REPAY: (Attach statements of income & expense)
Gross Income: $_____
_____% Vacancy $_____
Expenses $_____
Net Available for Debt Service $_____
Debt X Income:

PLACEMENT AGREEMENT

THIS AGREEMENT, entered into this ____ day of _____ 19____ by and between _____ herein referred to as PRINCIPAL and _____ herein referred to as CLIENT.

WHEREAS, the PRINCIPAL has developed investors who are desirous of making loans.

WHEREAS, the CLIENT is desirous of obtaining a loan in the amount of _____.

NOW THEREFORE, in consideration of mutual promises and agreements hereinafter set forth, the parties mutually agree as follows:

PRINCIPAL agrees to obtain a loan in the amount of _____ for a term of _____ with maximum interest being _____% for said CLIENT, providing this transaction is approved by the investor.

IN CONSIDERATION of services rendered, CLIENT agrees to pay PRINCIPAL a commission of _____% of the amount of loan at the time of loan approval.

CLIENT agrees to give PRINCIPAL an advance earnest deposit of money in the amount of _____, which will be held in escrow by PRINCIPAL for a maximum period of _____ days from above date and refunded to CLIENT at the end of this period or at the time of loan rejection or at the time of loan closing. Under no circumstances will PRINCIPAL hold said earnest deposit longer than __60__ days except in the event CLIENT shall violate or default on any provision of this agreement. and by this act of violation or default CLIENT waives all claims and rights to earnest deposit held by PRINCIPAL.

CLIENT agrees to pay PRINCIPAL an advance processing and placement fee of _____ in payment of expenses connected with loan such as: credit investigation, examination of deeds, titles, etc., which is not refundable.

THIS contract shall be considred honored and terminated when all promises and agreements herein stated have been fulfilled by all parties in good faith.

PRINCIPAL   CLIENT
By:_____   By:_____ title
In Witness:_____   By:_____ title

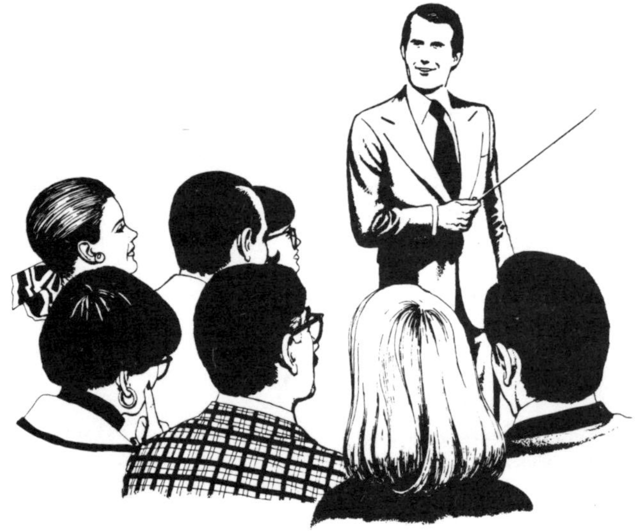

How to Start Your Own University for Under $50

Under the constitution of the United States it is quite easy to start your own university or college — especially if principles are based on a religious concept. The United States insures religious freedom and the church and the state are separate entities; the state does not support churches and the church does not contribute to the state government.

There are a number of universities and colleges offering home study courses and issuing diplomas, certificates and degrees that are valid anywhere in this country. The universities operate legally and even enjoy protection from the U.S. Congress that no federal or state government will interfere with the operation of the school. One of the first amendments of the United States declares: "Congress shall make no law regarding religious establishment or prohibiting the freedom to exercise thereof." There was also a law passed by the Supreme Court in 1970 stating that all religious institutions and the property that they own are tax exempt.

It is your right that you can establish a religion or church and appoint yourself as the minister. Also, you can issue diplomas to anyone or even to yourself ("Doctor of Philosophy" or any degree from a B.S. to a PhD). Your school or university may also charge fees for granting a degree to individuals who pass the minimum requirements that you establish. Many of the schools operate entirely by mail and receive $15,000 to $50,000 selling degrees. In most cases, there are practically no requirements to receive a diploma...fees range from $50 to $400 or more.

Here are the Steps for Starting Your Own University or College

First: Form your own corporation (non-profit) with the secretary of state in the same state where the school is to be located. Then go to a printer and have letterheads, business cards, and diplomas printed. Example:

Rev. Arthur J. Jamerson, PhD.
11220 South Main Street
San Francisco, California 90070

In most states, to become a minister you need only file with the county court house (Clerk's office). The fee is around $5 and you are legally a minister, able to perform marrige ceremonies, etc. Make sure to check local laws before performing these services.

Second: To gain tax exempt status, file an application with I.R.S. (a good CPA will show you how or you may call your local I.R.S. office, and they will be glad to send you all the pertinent papers).

Third: Join the National Association of Institutions of Religious Education. This will add prestige to your university.

Being the founder of a religious university and an ordained minister of the church adds to your status in the community. Also, many airlines, hotels, motels and clubs offer discounts to members of the church.

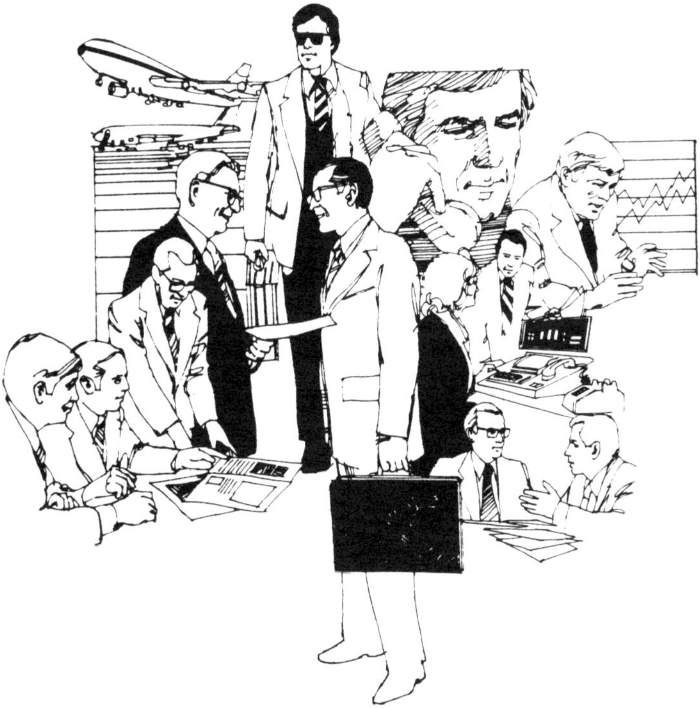

How to Completely Disappear and Change Your Identity

For various reasons, thousands of people every year may wish to change their identity and become another person. All identification begins with birth, a birth certificate, to be specific. Then, as you grow older, you obtain a driver's license, social security card, and a passport. Once you have all of these means of identification, you have solidly established your identity... supposedly!

This chapter is designed for the person who has overpowering personal problems... for the person who needs total escape, starting a new life and being able to be free of all past liabilities and debts.

Now, it is truly within your power to disappear and be completely free of all your past identification. Not only that, I will show you how your tracks can be covered so no one will ever be able to discover the new you. You will be reborn with a new identity and a new future.

The plan is simple, but it takes a little work on your part. The first means of new identification that you need is a birth certificate. To obtain a valid new birth certificate, you must find someone who has passed away in a major city like New York, Chicago or Los Angeles. Make sure that the person was the same race and sex and born in the same year as you. You can find this information in any city newspaper obituary column on file in a public library. Pick out several who seem likely to fill your requirements. Be sure to note the place of birth.

Once you have researched and found a name, age, sex and race that meets your requirements (and have the place of birth), write to the court house where the person was born requesting a certified copy of "Your new birth certificate" telling them that you lost your original copy. It is probably a good idea to send along a business card with your "new" name printed on it, maybe even on your "new" personal stationery. Once you have received your new birth certificate, you are on your way to establishing a new identity.

Now that you have a new birth certificate, you need to apply for a social security number. If you have any problem getting one, you can tell them that you did odd jobs in New York City and never had a need for one, but since you are getting older you felt that you may need the benefits when you retire. The same can apply for the driver's license you will need to apply for to complete the identification. About 25% of all the people who live in New York City have never driven. So, the fact that you have never driven will not raise any eyebrows. You should have no problem seeking new employment in another state, and taking advantage of your new future. "Nice to make your new acquaintance!"

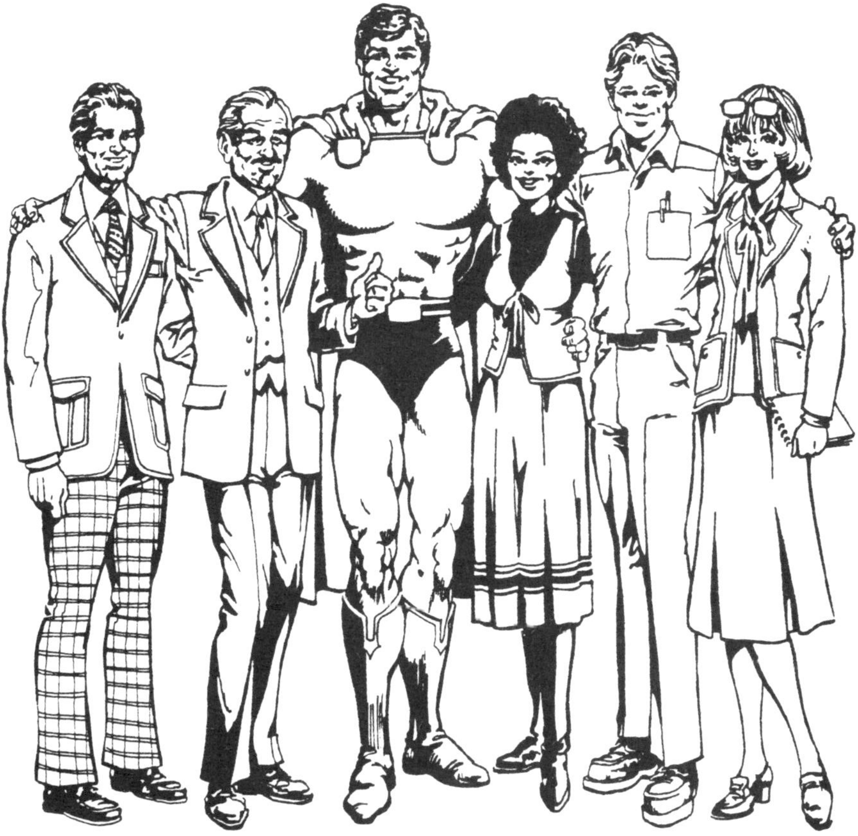

Get V.I.P. Treatment

You don't have to be a Movie Star!
You don't have to be a TV personality!
You don't have to be a state Senator!

What you have to be is yourself, the real you! Anyone can appear to be wealthy. It is just a matter of having the right credentials, moving into the right circles and meeting and knowing the right people. Doing this will get you V.I.P. treatment wherever you go and whatever you do.

One of the easiest ways to form this image is to start your own hometown newspaper, you being the editor, or the sports columnist, or even the restaurant critic.

Have three hundred business cards printed (one-third as Editor, one-third as the sports writer, and one-third as the restaurant critic for your hometown Herald Examiner).

Once you have created this image, you will be treated like Royalty with the respect due an important newspaper editor. Giving the appearance of being a wealthy newspaper owner will give you the V.I.P. treatment you have always wanted.

By using this maneuver, you will be able to receive the following:

Editor . . . . special events, plays, theaters. You will get the best seats in the house. Free!

Sports Writer . . . . football games, baseball, any sporting events you will choose. Tickets for you and your friends. Free!

Restaurant Gourmet . . . . you will have your choice to dine in the best restaurant in town. Free!

You will also be able to receive free hotel reservations in famous or little known resorts in all parts of the country. Drop them a line informing them that you have been commissioned to do an article on the resort with pictures and a full page display. See how fast you can enjoy all kinds of vacations. Free of charge.

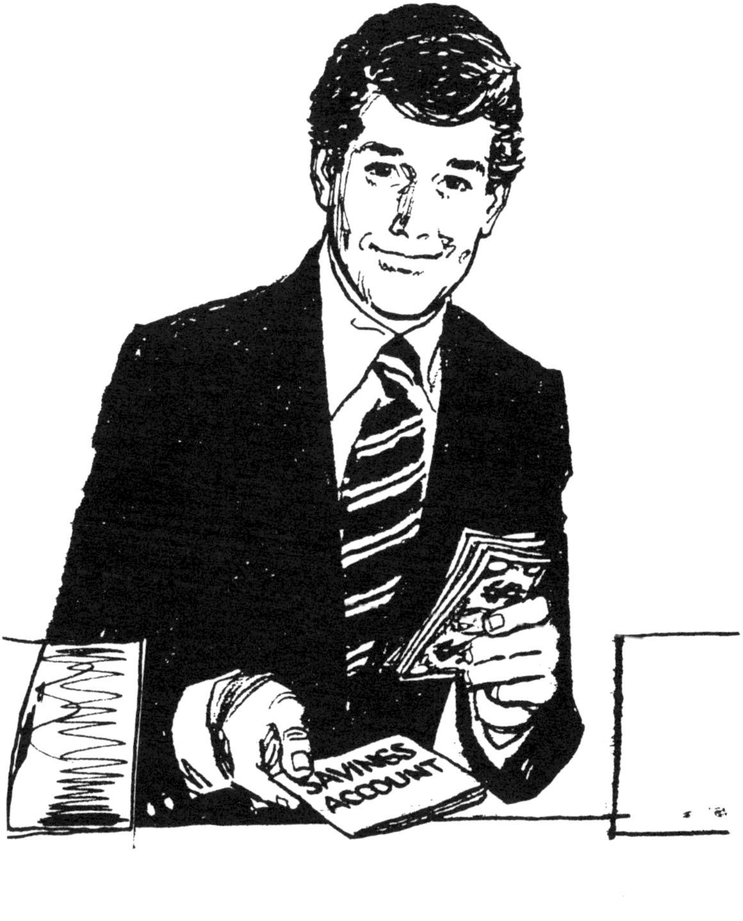
SAVINGS
ACCOUNT

Stop Paying Taxes...Legally

Following a few easy steps you will be free from taxes for the rest of your life.

You will be exempt from paying:
> Federal Income Tax!
> State Income Tax!
> Personal Property Tax!
> Sales Tax!

The Internal Revenue Service has admitted that millions of Americans can set up churches and avoid paying income taxes. A spokesman for I.R.S. admits that there is a loophole in the tax system and they are stymied in their efforts to halt people from avoiding taxes.

If you wish to take advantage of this plan, form a church and appoint yourself as minister. To make sure that you are abiding by all the state and federal laws, you should contact an attorney who is familiar with I.R.S. regulations. For a small fee he will insure that you are not breaking any laws.

These are the Steps Required to Become Tax Exempt

1. Become an ordained minister of an accepted religion. The National College of Arts and Sciences has a program whereby you can become an ordained minister in less than two weeks. Write: Chancellor's Office, P.O. Box 2356, Tulsa, Oklahoma 74101. Fee: $125.00.
2. Form a corporation and file the name of your church with your county Clerk's Office.
3. After forming the corporation, you must turn over all of your income to the church and deduct a tax exempt salary as the minister. Contact your nearest I.R.S. office for eligibility forms.
4. Open a checking account in the corporation's name (name of church). In this way you will be able to operate your personal business under a tax exempt status.

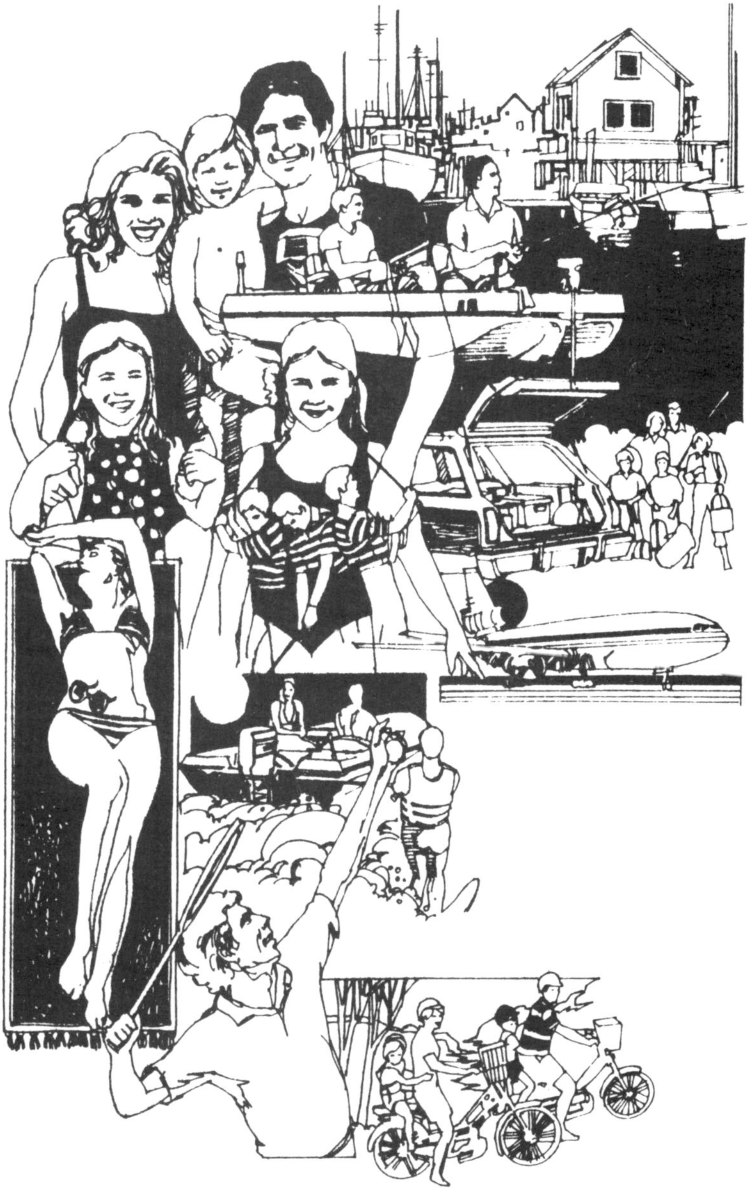

Raise $5,000 in Cash on Your Credit Cards

There are certain times in everyone's life when a person needs to raise cash...fast. And if you have over-extended yourself with all the local banks, you face the problem of finding a source for a loan.

If you read the chapter titled, "Carry all the Major Credit Cards You Want," chances are that you have at least Bankamericard and Master Charge or maybe even the American Express credit cards. However, if the only ones you have so far are Master Charge and Visa, let me show you how easy it is to raise $5,000.

In most states there is more than one bank representing Master Charge and Bankamericard. If you look in the yellow pages, you will find at least ten different banks offering these charge cards. Once you have received approval from one of the banks, you will have no difficulty in obtaining Master Charge and Visa cards from each one of them. For each bank it is its business to make interest on the purchases you make by using their cards only. The banks have a ceiling on each card up to $500, so if you received cards from ten different banks you would have a ceiling of $5,000. The ceiling on the credit cards is not only for store purchases but you can receive up to $500 cash on each, by going straight to the banks and presenting your card. It's that simple. They will extend you the cash on the spot.

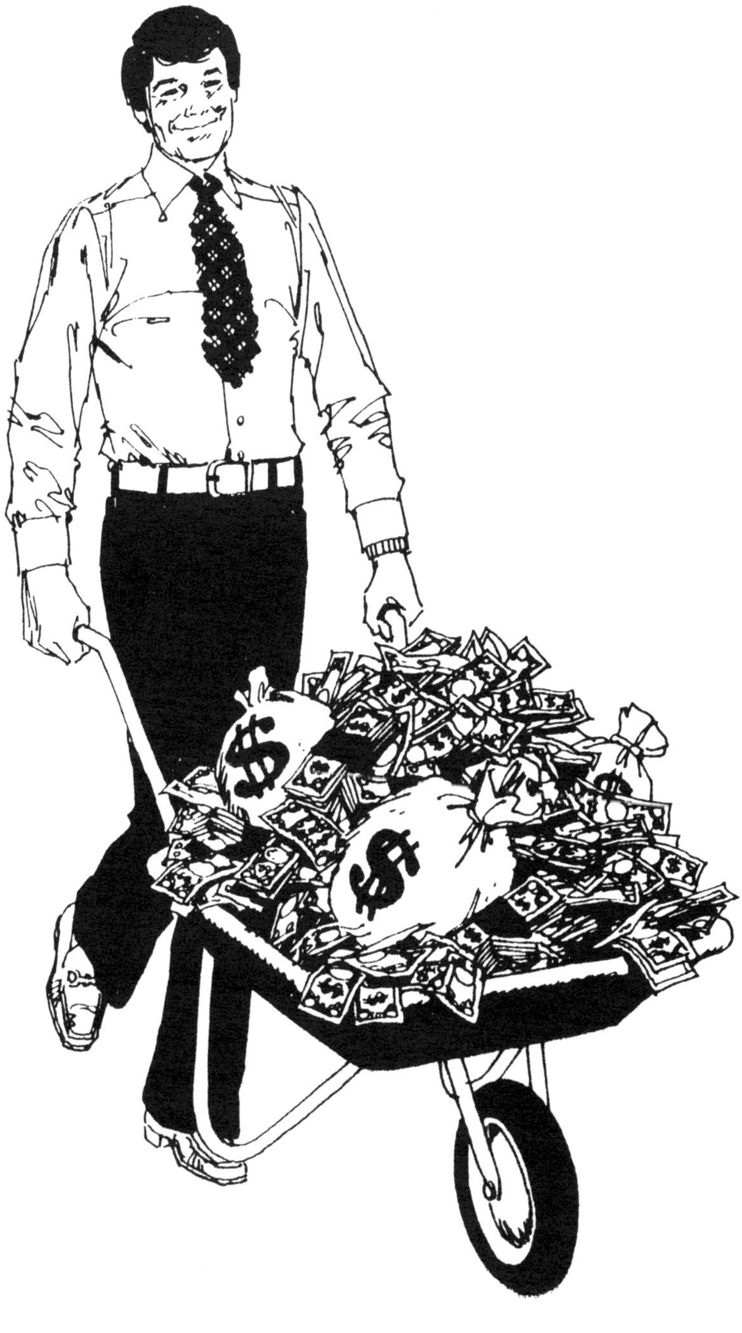

Own a Million Dollar Corporation

The easiest way to acquire a million dollar corporation is to file a Certificte of Incorporation in the state of Delaware as shown in the chapter, "How to Form a Corporation." After you have received your Certificate of Incorporation, file an amendment with the state of Delaware. Send it to the attention of the Secretary of State, Department of Incorporation, Dover, Delaware 19901.

In filing the amendment, change the original par value that you set for your capitalization to $100, and by issuing 10,000 shares of stock, you have become the president of a million dollar corporation.

You will receive no opposition from the state of Delaware for under the laws of forming a corporation, there is no restriction on the amount of capital. The state of Delaware does not require you or the corporation to prove capitalization.

By filing this amendment, you have become a millionaire. However, I must warn you that it is fraudulent if you use this corporation to receive a loan. Always check with your CPA before issuing a financial statement for the purpose of obtaining credit of any amount.

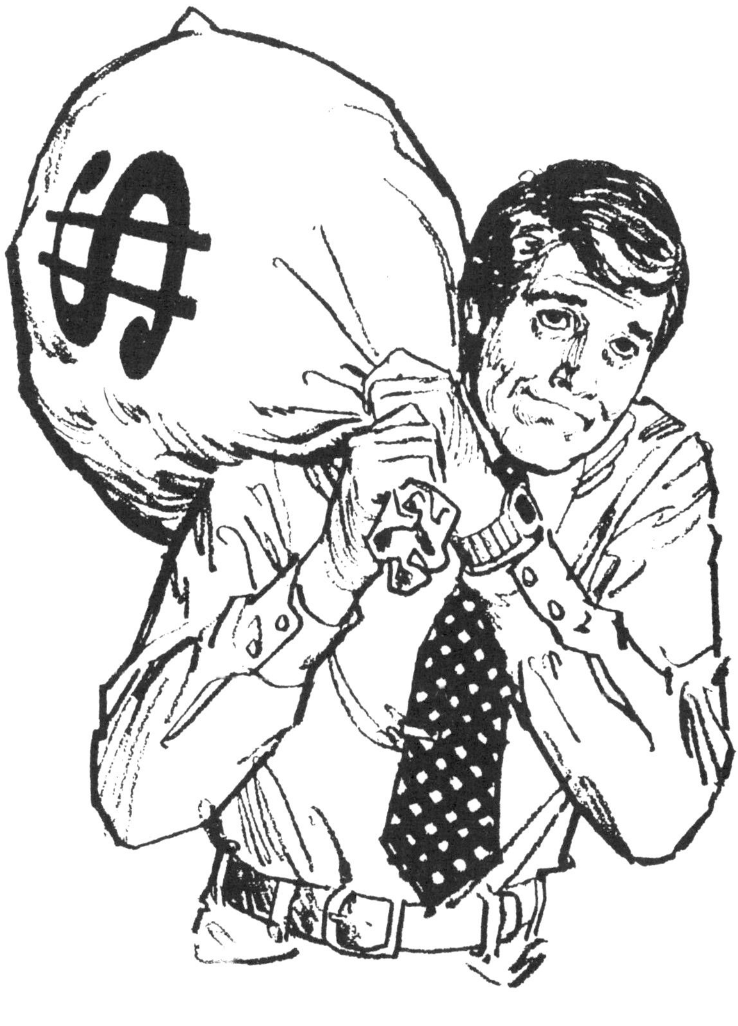

Loans, Capital, Mortgages, from $1,000 to $250,000

In this chapter I am going to show ten ways to borrow from $1000 to $250,000 on just your signature.

Plan One

There are several lending companies who advertise that they will loan up to $25,000 on your signature with NO CREDIT INVESTIGATION. Here is a list of the companies. Write to them requesting an application.

Nationwide Finance Corp.
Suite 927, 1660 S. Albion St.
Denver, CO 80222

Commercial Credit Corp.
55 Madison Avenue
New York, NY 10022
212-679-7725

Finance America VIP
2917 S. Western Ave.
Oklahoma City, OK 73109
405-631-4401

Avco Colorado Industrial Bank
P.O. Box 31225
Los Angeles, CA 90031

Dial Finance Corp.
2007 S. Main Street
P.O. Box 2321
Santa Ana, CA 92717
714-556-0810

Postal Thrift Loans
703 Douglas Street
Sioux City, IA 51102

Beneficial Executive Loan Service
2858 Stevens Creek Blvd.
San Jose, CA 95128
800-538-6811

C.I.T. Financial Corp.
650 Madison Avenue
New York, NY 10022
212-572-6500

Capital Financial Services
Ste. 208, 1930 S. Hill St.
Oceanside, CA 92054

S.F.C.
1561 S. Green River Road
Evansville, IN 47715

Plan Two

Here is another way to borrow just on your signature alone. In this country there are hundreds of banks who are offering overdraft privileges to their customers who have a checking account with them, regardless if you reside in their state or not.

To qualify for the loan, you must have an open checking account with them, and apply for the overdraft privilege with a separate loan application.

An overdraft account is where the customer can write a bad check up to sometimes as high as $50,000, and the bank automatically covers any check you write up to the limit of the overdraft privilege.

To find these banks offering this overdraft protection, I advise that you use your local and out-of-state yellow page directories. You will find the ones offering overdraft protection advertising as such in their ads. Just drop them a line stating that you request an application for a checking account with their bank and for them also to send along an application for overdraft protection. You will find them easy to do business with as long as you open a checking account and then you wait until the permanent checks arrive, not the temporary checks you will receive first.

Plan Three

If you find that you are having trouble securing a loan through local sources, you can apply for a Small Business loan from the Small Business Administration. They have a few requirements before they will approve the application one being that you have been turned down by at least two lending institutions and second, that you have business experience in the venture that you have chosen. If it is a restaurant, let's say, you must have worked in one, preferably as a manager. Or if it is a retail business that you are interested in, then you must be familiar with all aspects of the business, from buying to selling, etc. etc.

The SBA will provide you with a loan to start virtually any new business at reasonable interest rates. The loans range from $2000 to $250,000, and anyone can qualify for their loans. There are no restrictions and in some cases, you can qualify for up to $20,000 with No Collateral.

For complete information write: Small Business Administration, 1444 L Street, N.W., Washington, DC 20005.

Plan Four

$15,000 worth of personal loans can be acquired by using the following method.

1. Apply for a $3000 personal loan from five different finance companies.
2. Fill out and mail each application the same day. Very important!
3. After receiving the $15,000, make an investment to cover the payments, and a little left over for yourself. Example: $3000 borrowed for 36 months, payments $120 per month. $120 x 5 = $600 per month.

   If you invest $15,000 in a restaurant as a silent partner, for instance, you should receive an income of at least $700 per month.
4. After finding a good investment, start the process all over again.

Plan Five

If you used the plan on how to carry all the major credit cards, you should have at least 20 cards by now. Mos credit cards carry a $500 limit on each card, and American Express and Diners carry up to $20,000 each if you apply for the additional limit. Here is the plan. Charge merchandise on your credit card and resell it for cash. This will give you the investment capital you need.

1. Go to your local department stores and charge gift certificates; afterward sell them to your fellow employees for less than the face value.
2. Apply at the airlines for a trip leaving in about 60 days. This way, you will receive at least 50% off. Once you have the ticket run an ad in the newspaper about 15 days before departure, advertising the tickets for less than normal air fare.

If you use this plan, and if you offer the merchandise at 15-20% discount, you must make more than that with your investment to cover the cost of the merchandise.

Plan Six

Another source for getting capital or cash loans is from foundations. With a solid business venture backed by research and planning, you will have more than a good chance of getting a loan, or an outright gift from $5000 up to $2,000,000.

I will furnish you a list of foundations in the United States offering Venture Capital for New Businesses, at the end of this chapter.

Plan Seven

Offering stock in your corporation is a form of borrowing to start your business venture. Some people I have known in the past have sold stock in their company before they even started in the business. There is only one drawback, and that is that you are not allowed to sell to more than 25 people or you must file your company with the Securities and Exchange Commission; and, that everyone you sell to must reside in the same state as your corporation. The only exception is if you incorporate in the state of Delaware. That is the only state without a S.E.C. office.

Plan Eight

If you are planning to buy a business, the Sale-Leaseback method will enable you to borrow cash on the equipment, and lease it back to yourself. This method works especially well if you are short of cash for the initial down payment. I will list some of the companies that specialize in Sale-Leaseback at the end of this chapter.

Plan Nine

Apply for a business loan out of the country. There are several European and Swiss banks offering loans to businessmen. These banks usually require that you have a checking account with them before they will consider your loan application. Here are a few which I recommend. Your local library should carry a complete list under "European Banking."

Swiss Credit Bank
Paradelatz
8022 Zurich, Switzerland

Swiss Bank Corporation
Aesschenvorstadt 1
4002 Basel, Switzerland

Amsterdam Rotterdam Bank
P.O. Box 1220
Amsterdam 1000, Holland

Pinansbanken
P.O. Box 298
DK 1501, Copenhagen V, Denmark

Plan Ten

Already I have shown you several methods to increase your borrowing power even if you have bad credit or have been bankrupt in the past. This final method will require you to prepare a written plan to submit to your co-signer. That's right, a co-signer. It's not against the law to pay a co-signer to sign for your loan, and in most cases they will be more than happy to if you have an interesting business venture.

SALE-LEASEBACK...VENTURE CAPITAL

Bea Associates, Inc.
366 Madison Ave.
New York, NY 10017

Brittany Capital Corp.
4325 R. N. B. Tower
Dallas, TX 75201

Cambridge Banking Partners
1711 Security Life Bldg.
Denver, CO 80202

Catawba Capital Corp.
Box 3121
Charlotte, NC 28203

David Morgenthaler
1033 National City Bank Bldg.
Cleveland, OH 44144

Developers Equity Co.
9348 Santa Monica Blvd.
Beverly Hills, CA 90210

Technimetrics, Inc.
527 Madison Avenue
New York, NY 10022

Explorer Fund, Inc.
28 State St.
Boston, MA 02109

Financial Resources, Inc.
1909 Storick Bldg.
Memphis, TN 38103

International Capital Corp.
800 Dorchester W.
Montreal 113, Que, Canada

General Pacific Investments
321 10th Street
San Francisco, CA 94103

Growth Equities, Ltd.
2116 Financial Center
Des Moines, IA 50309

Intercom Investment Co.
100 S. Wacker Dr.
Chicago, IL 60606

Kalb Voorhis and Company
27 William St.
New York, NY 10005

Mid Tex Capital Corp.
104 North Ave. E.
Clifton, TX 76634

National Lead Company
111 Broadway
New York, NY 10006

Home Life Insurance Co.
253 Broadway
New York, NY 10007

Continental Assurance Co.
310 S. Michigan Ave.
Chicago, IL 60604

D. D. Cantor Associates
25 S. Service Rd.
Jericho, NY 11723

Emil Mosbacher
515 Madison Ave.
New York, NY 10022

Life and Casualty Inc. Co.
Life and Casualty Tower
Nashville, TN 37219

Nationwide Development Co.
246 N. High St.
Columbus, OH 43215

Philip Fogel Company
51 Elm St.
Englewood Cliff, NJ 07632

Ruhl and Ruhl, Inc.
First National Bldg.
Davenport, IA 52801

The Kempner Corp.
60 E. 42nd St.
New York, NY 10017

Paine Venture Fund
Box 73
Boston, MA 02110

Professional SBIC
5979 W. 3rd St.
Los Angeles, CA 90036

Hanover Small Business Investment
Box 747
Charlotte, NC 28231

Loeb, Rhodes and Company
42 Wall St.
New York, NY 10005

Montag and Caldwell, Inc.
2901 1st National Bank Tower
Atlanta, GA 30303

North Star Industries
4570 W. 77th St.
Minneapolis, MN 55435

Central Manufacturing District
1 First National Plaza
Chicago, IL 60670

Connecticut Mutual Life Insurance
140 Garden St.
Hartford, CT 06105

City Center Real Estate
919 3rd Ave.
New York, NY 10016

Gibson Willoughby, Ltd.
100 University Ave.
Toronto, Ont., Canada

Mutual Life Insurance Co.
1740 Broadway
New York, NY 10019

Penn Mutual Life Insurance
530 Walnut St.
Philadelphia, PA 15222

Prudential Life Insurance Co.
Prudential Mall
Newark, NJ 07102

State Mutual Life Assurance
440 Lincoln St.
Worcester, MA 01605

Travelers Insurance
Securities Department
Hartford, CT 06115

Pan American Capital Corp.
24 Commerce St.
Newark, NJ 07102

R. and D. Capital Co.
2700 Merced St.
San Leandro, CA 9457

Research Industries, Inc.
123 N. Pitt St. Ste. A201
Alexandria, VA

Rockefeller Brothers, Inc.
30 Rockefeller Plaza
New York, NY 10020

Standard Growth Capital
Box 10106
Knoxville, TN 37919

Technology Search Associates
1 Spruce Hill Rd.
Weston, MA 02193

U.A.G. Investment Corp.
Box 67
Robesonia, PA 1951

Vanguard Venture Capital
301 E. Main St.
Barrington, IL 60010

Venture Investments Corp.
714 N. Valley Mills Dr.
Waco, TX 76710

Western Group, Inc.
Box 1273
Weston, CT 06880

Wilshire Capital Corp.
10000 Santa Monica Blvd.
Los Angeles, CA 90067

Cross Trust
95 N. Main St.
Concord, NH

Ohio Brass Foundation
380 North Main St.
Mansfield, OH 44902

Tabas Family Foundation
915 N. Delaware Ave.
Philadelphia, PA 19123

FOUNDATIONS
Melrose Foundation, Inc.
Washington Ave & Mitchell St.
Knoxville, TN 37917

Gregory Charitable Trust
Box 2558
Houston, TX 77001

Bostwick Foundation, Inc.
Shelburne, VT

Resources and Tech. Mgt. Co.
Box 100
Chestnut Hill, MA 02167

Russ and Company
Alamo National Bldg.
San Antonio, TX 78205

State Street Bank Company
225 Franklin St.
Boston, MA 02101

TFK Corporation
Orosi, CA 93647

Union Commerce Capital
Box 5876
Cleveland, OH 44101

Venture Capital Corp.
540 Frontage Rd.
Northfield, IL 60093

Wall Street Venture Capital
2 Esterbrook Lane
Cherry Hill, NJ 08002

William Blair and Company
135 S. LaSalle St.
Chicago, IL 60603

Cobb Foundation
802 1st National Bank Bldg.
Great Falls, MT 59401

Battle Foundation, Inc.
Box 1240
Rocky Mount, NC

Otasco Foundation
6901 East Pine St.
Tulsa, OK 74101

Grinnell Fund
Old Hartford Pike
North Scituate, RI

Hatterscheidt Foundation, Inc.
302 Capitol Bldg.
Aberdeen, SD 57401

Bamberger Memorial Foundation
1401 Walker Bank Bldg.
Salt Lake City, UT 84111

Public Welfare Foundation
Washington, VA

Jackson Foundation
Box 240
St. Thomas, VI

Woodbridge-Brown Fund
Box 1793
Charleston, WV 25326

Wehu Foundation, Inc.
2100 Marine Plaza
Milwaukee, WI 53202

Cowles Foundation, Inc.
601 Chronicle Bldg.
Spokane, WA 99201

Keesee Educational Fund, Inc.
Box 226
Martinville, VA 24112

De Rance, Inc.
324 North 76th St.
Milwaukee, WI 53213

Matson Trust
Boyd Bldg. Suite 618
Cheyenne, WY 82001